THE SCHOOL OF GRIEF

PRAISE FOR *THE SCHOOL OF GRIEF*

I've read dozens of highly recommended good books on grief. *The School of Grief* is by far the best. Nothing comes close. Nothing. Raw tender transparency. Thoroughly researched, yet an easy captivating read. Powerful, not preachy. Comprehensive with an amazing economy of words. I bought a dozen of these books to give to others in grief. I know I will be giving away many more. I'm confident you will do the same.
Dr. David W. Miller, Pastor and Consultant

With a heart for Jesus, the love of a parent, the insight of a grief educator, and the wisdom of a pastor, my friend David Page guides us through the process of grief so we can find hope. *The School of Grief* is a must-have resource for anyone wanting to grow through loss and tragedy.
Caleb Kaltenbach, Research Pastor at Shepherd Church and Author of *Messy Grace*

The School of Grief is excellent in providing deeper understanding around healing, enabling the grieving soul to find hope in a new life, a different life, but one that is good, rich, and purposeful. This book is full of wonderfully rich nuggets of wisdom, encouragement and practical perspectives that can only come from a person who knows and has lived through profound loss.
Jennifer Norheim LMFT, Pastor of Counseling at Saddleback Church

The School of Grief will help you begin the healing process when your life seems unbearable. It will assist you in lifting the cloud of hopelessness and aid you in finding true JOY once again. Besides the Bible itself, I don't know of a better book to read when your pain seems unending.
Dudley Rutherford, Lead Pastor at Shepherd Church

As a pastor, I appreciate Dave's heart to help people in pain. I've had the privilege of working with Dave and seeing him walk beside others on their grief journey and help them turn their pain into purpose. *The School of Grief* will help you mend your broken heart and put the pieces of your life back together after your loss. I highly recommend it.
Andy Wood, Lead Pastor at Saddleback Church

Dave is a man of deep faith, who suffered a great loss yet had joy in his life. I witnessed his joy time and time again as he ministered to those around him. This book is filled with wisdom, born out of painstaking loss, and is a powerful example of the truth that God desires to recycle our pain. A vast resource for people facing life at its worst, this book can help lead you to life again.
Ron Sylvia, Lead Pastor at Church @ The Springs

This book is an invaluable companion for those navigating grief and for those supporting them. Through his personal journey, Dave guides readers to recognize their own needs and grow through grief. Skillfully blending scripture and storytelling, the book offers an honest view of the grieving process. Having recently lost my mom, Dave's book has brought immense comfort by giving words to my experiences and helping others understand my needs during different stages of grief.
Linda Tokar, Spiritual Growth Pastor at Saddleback Church

The School of Grief shows us how to regain hope, meaning, and purpose following a major loss. Whatever type of loss you've faced in the past or are facing today, this book is for you. Losses must be grieved, and this book will help you do so in ways that are redemptive for the future.
Dr. Gary L. McIntosh, Distinguished Professor at Talbot School of Theology

For anyone grieving who wants their soul and spirit restored, who doesn't understand the purpose of their loss, who yearns for hope, this book is for you. Dave provides compassionate guidance, effective tools, and comfort for those in the School of Grief. This book is a clear, concise, and practical guide on the grieving process.
Rex Minor, Pastor of Support Groups at Saddleback Church

I highly recommend this book for anyone who is grieving a loss and trying to find a way to move forward. Where you hang your hat spiritually matters. This book offers a faith-based approach to healing, reminding readers they can lean on God for strength. Dr. Page offers practical advice and spiritual insights to help readers find hope and healing when they need it the most.
Pam Vetter, Los Angeles Funeral Celebrant

During seasons of loss, we look for a safe place to anchor our thoughts and emotions so we can process them well. This book provides such a place. I found the words to be a safe harbor where the waves of grief can be gently navigated, and hope is found in God who calms our storms.
Deanna Emick, Care Pastor at Saddleback Church

The School of Grief is a masterpiece resource guide on one of the most overlooked emotions that human beings face. This book is the most helpful, powerful, and meaningful guidebook that a person facing catastrophic loss could ever read. Every church and counseling center should have this book available to support those facing any storm.
Halie O'Ryan, Singer and Songwriter

The School of Grief provides thoughtful guidance on how to navigate loss. As a trainer of counselors and ministry leaders, I incorporate Dr. Page's tools into my lessons on grief and loss because it provides practical guidance that is valuable for all servant leaders. Dr. Page reminds us that we are not alone in our grief, and we can all provide comfort through a loving presence.
Chris Clark, Care Pastor at Saddleback Church

THE SCHOOL OF GRIEF

A Guide to Finding Hope, Meaning and Purpose After Loss

Dr. David Page

Copyright © 2023 by Dr. David Page

School of Grief Publishing

All Rights Reserved

For my family:

To my wife, Carrie, my partner in life and ministry,

To my children, Joshua, Jessica, and Jackie,

my daughter in heaven and

inspiration on earth.

Table of Contents

Preface 10

Introduction 13

PART ONE: MY STORY 16

Chapter 1:
Jumping Into Daddy's Arms 17

Chapter 2:
The Day My Daughter Died 31

Chapter 3:
Will Life Ever Be Good Again? 39

PART TWO: UNDERSTANDING GRIEF 45

Chapter 4:
What Is Grief? 46

Chapter 5:
Models Of Grief 61

Chapter 6:
The Best And Worst Things To Say 69

Chapter 7:
Faith And Grief 83

PART THREE: THE SEVEN NEEDS OF THE GRIEVING 95

Chapter 8:
The Seven Needs Of The Grieving 96

Chapter 9:
To Have Your Grief Witnessed 101

Chapter 10:
To Feel Your Feelings 122

Chapter 11:
To Release Your Burden Of Guilt 137

Chapter 12:
To Face Your Fears 147

Chapter 13:
To Not Get Over It – But Grow Into It 154

Chapter 14:
To Turn Your Pain Into Purpose 162

Chapter 15:
To Hold Onto The Hope Of Heaven 175

Endnotes 189

Translations 193

About the Author 194

PREFACE

Who is this book for?

This book is a comprehensive resource designed to support anyone who has experienced loss, primarily those who have lost a loved one. Whether you have lost a spouse, child, sibling, extended relative or friend, this book offers solace and assistance during your grieving process.

This book is for anyone who yearns for hope, is weary and in need of soul restoration, is searching for a renewed sense of purpose, is stuck and can't find a way forward, and who recognizes the importance of grieving alongside others on similar paths.

This guide also extends its relevance beyond the realm of bereavement. It is valuable for those facing other forms of loss and difficult life transitions. Whether you are navigating the challenges of a divorce, a miscarriage, a financial loss, pet loss, the death of a dream, coping with the emotional toll of a job loss or retirement, dealing with trauma, surviving a suicide loss, or confronting a terminal illness, this book aims to provide support and guidance in your unique circumstances.

This book is also for you if you are looking for tools to help and support others on their grief journey. You are in the right place if you are a counselor, therapist, teacher, coach, celebrant, clergy member, social worker, health care or mental health professional, hospice worker, first responder, police officer, behavior support specialist, or grief educator.

Why did I write this book?

I penned this book because of a deep calling and profound sense of purpose to help individuals traversing the difficult path of grief, extending a compassionate hand to those in mourning. My goal was to create and share a compassionate guide for individuals who have endured profound loss, aimed at providing comfort and support to those who need it the most. I wanted a book I could give to anyone who's experienced loss, whether it was a loss that occurred last week, last year, or a lifetime ago.

However, the most compelling motivation and qualification for writing this book lies in the existence of my cherished daughter, Jackie. Deliberately avoiding the past tense, I always refrain from stating, "I once had a daughter named Jackie." I still have a connection with my daughter and talk about her all the time. Although she is not earth-bound, she is still very much present in my mind, heart, and soul. When people ask how many children I have, I answer, "Three. Two on earth, and one in heaven." I'll always have three kids. My grief for her never ends because my love never ends.

I have personally experienced grief. I have skin in the game. I am a father who lost his youngest child to a brain tumor when she was just five years old. I understand how different our lives become after loss. I know the excruciating pain of losing a child and being in this world without Jackie. It hurts to bury your child. No parent should ever have to undergo such a traumatic experience. She should have lived to bury me.

I wrote this book because I have a compelling story to tell. I share about grief and the seven needs of grieving people. I offer insight from a father's perspective. This isn't just a book about grief; it's a love story between a father and daughter and the lessons Jackie has taught me about life, death, and the afterlife. In these pages, I reveal the tears, trials, and triumphs that I've experienced on my unique grief journey.

This book represents thousands of hours of being in the trenches with grieving people and offering care and comfort during the most painful times in their lives. This includes leading a grief community, grief retreats, grief training courses, grief counseling, and performing Celebration of Life services.

I remember my daughter with much more love than pain. I have a sorrowful soul yet am filled with joy each day. I have dedicated the rest of my life to helping grieving people and educating our grief illiterate world about grief. I have a passion to help people find their smile again after loss. That's why I wrote this book.

INTRODUCTION

Welcome to the School of Grief, a unique and inclusive community that transcends traditional notions of education. There are no physical classrooms, principals, or homework assignments.

> The School of Grief is for…
> The brokenhearted.
> The grievers.
> The mourners.
> The lamenters.
> The ones who have been robbed of a loved one.

I am so sorry for your loss and wish I could offer a comforting hug.

Losing a loved one is one of the most formidable challenges we encounter, but it is possible to navigate life without them and discover hope, meaning, and purpose in a way that honors their memory.

In the School of Grief, we provide a space where you have permission to grieve—a haven where we won't judge or take away your grief. You were created with the capacity to grieve, and it is a gift from God to help you navigate life's transitions. Grief is a pathway to healing your broken heart, and in this school, we honor and embrace that process.

In the School of Grief, we acknowledge that each person's grief is as unique as a fingerprint. However, what we all share is the fundamental need to have our grief witnessed. We respect and honor every individual's grief journey. Here, you will never be told to "get over" your grief or to "move on." Each of us experiences grief in our own way and in our own time. There is no set timeline or expectation. Instead, we grow into our grief and find ways to live with it.

In the School of Grief, you will learn a faith-based approach to grief and the importance of leaning on God for strength. Jesus serves as our ultimate model for grief, as he himself was "a man of sorrows and acquainted with grief" (Isaiah 53:3). He understands our despair and stands with us in our pain. He showed us that it is okay to grieve, to shed tears, and to express our emotions.

The shortest verse in the Bible simply says, "Jesus wept" (John 11:35). In this school, we value tears as a natural part of the grieving process. We grieve fully, but unlike those without hope, we find our hope in Jesus—the source of our comfort and optimism. He offers us hope both in the present and the future.

I entered the School of Grief two decades ago, after the loss of my precious daughter. Like you, my life was forever changed by my loss. As a fellow griever, I have committed the remainder of my life to helping those who grieve, generously sharing the compassion and solace I personally received from my higher power with those in need. A higher power is some-

INTRODUCTION

thing greater than us. God is my higher power. Having faith in a higher power can assist your healing.

We live in a society that often lacks understanding and literacy about grief. As a grief educator and pastor, I am committed to teaching you about grief and the seven needs of grieving, equipping you with the necessary tools to heal your own heart so you can guide others on their unique grief journeys.

In the School of Grief, we recognize that we belong to a timeless community of mourners that stretches back thousands of years and continues to this day. We long for our heavenly home and the day when we will be reunited with our loved ones. For now, we wrestle with the paradox of pain and proclaim that God is good, that He draws near to the brokenhearted, and that nothing can separate us from His love.

We will embark on a path of healing, resilience, and growth, holding onto our cherished memories while forging a new path forward, embracing life with open hearts and renewed purpose.

I invite you to enroll with me in the School of Grief.

You are not alone.

Turn the page and let's get started together in the School of Grief.

PART ONE:
MY STORY

CHAPTER 1:
JUMPING INTO DADDY'S ARMS

> *"We do not remember days, we remember moments."*
> Cesare Pavese

A Moment in Time

Have you ever experienced a moment you wished you could freeze in time?

As I pulled my car into our driveway, I could hear my little girl's scream echoing through the neighborhood, "Daddy's home! Daddy's home!" I looked up to see my five-year-old daughter, Jackie, bounding down the stairs of our deck to greet me.

As I opened my car door and stood, she took a flying leap and jumped into my arms. I caught her, held her, and kissed her little head, never realizing what a cherished memory this moment would become. This wasn't a one-time announcement to the neighborhood but a regular ritual that occurred each day during the work week. I wish I could freeze that moment and hold onto it forevermore. I would give anything to hear those words again. I believe someday I will.

What makes this moment so memorable was the sequence of events that followed shortly thereafter. Jackie, who could light up any room with her smile, was now experiencing unusual symptoms that a battery of tests couldn't explain. An MRI finally revealed an inoperable brain tumor. She died in my arms six weeks later, but the emotional aftershocks still linger. My heart was broken in a way I never imagined possible. This was a turning point that changed the course of my life as I took my first steps on a lifelong grief journey. Yet, out of the darkness, my deepest life purpose would emerge from the rubble of my pain.

I can't escape the pain of missing those happy moments and I don't want to. I do more than just treasure those special times. I long for them, I savor them, and I thank God for them. I close my eyes and picture her running down the stairs with a huge smile on her face as she leaps into my arms. That memory will forever be engraved in my brain. I remember her with more love than pain and for that, I am thankful. My grief for Jackie will never end because my love for her will never end.

On Top of the World

I was on top of the world. Our family recently moved from Southern California to Auburn, CA to start a church. Auburn is a beautiful suburb of Sacramento, located in the Sierra Foothills on the way to Lake Tahoe. My marriage to Carrie was at an all-time high and our three young children were doing well in school. My wife found a job she enjoyed, where she spent her time working with kids with autism. I was pastoring an exciting, fast-growing church, which was only four years old yet already had eight hundred people attending each Sunday. Life was good. It seemed my future and our family's future were bright.

When Your World Comes Crashing Down

It was the beginning of a new millennium. Jackie was in preschool and was slated to begin kindergarten in the fall. On New Year's Day, I participated in the polar bear swim at Lake of the Pines in Auburn. The water temperature in the lake was 42 degrees. The whole family came to watch me compete, but Jackie lagged behind. We were in the minivan ready to go, when we noticed Jackie crying, as she clung to the rail on our deck, slowly making her way down the stairs.

"Jackie, hurry up. We're going to be late," Carrie said. Jackie cried even louder. "What's wrong?" Carrie asked empathetically.

"I don't know, Mommy," Jackie replied. She got in the minivan, and we headed to the lake. That was our first clue indicating that something wasn't right.

A few days later, we noticed a little drool coming from the side of her mouth. We weren't sure what it was. Carrie wiped it off, but it continued at various times throughout the day.

A few days later, I took Jessica, my other daughter, and Jackie shopping for an Easter dress. While skimming through hangers, Jackie fell into a rack of dresses. As I pulled the clothes apart, I found her on the floor looking up at me, laughing. She stood and we continued shopping, but I knew something was wrong. Her gait was off. Jackie ran everywhere she went and now her balance was compromised.

We decided to take her to the doctor to see what was going on. My wife took her to Kaiser Permanente, and they checked her out and took a blood sample. They told us everything was fine, that she most likely had a viral infection but that it was nothing to worry about. They also said sometimes kids who were around the age of five could regress and begin to drool. But the symptoms didn't go away. They got worse. They ran more tests, including a CAT scan and spinal tap. All the tests came back negative, and they assured us that Jackie was fine. But we knew in our hearts she wasn't. We asked if there were any more tests they could run to see what was going on. The only test left was an MRI.

We scheduled an MRI for the following week. MRIs are very intimidating for a five-year-old child. Carrie got into the MRI machine and went through the scan with her so that she wouldn't be afraid. I was present for the MRI, and then a friend picked me up at the hospital and drove me to the Sacramento airport to catch a plane for Los Angeles. I was speaking at a Saddleback Church conference with Rick Warren the following day.

Diagnosis and Prognosis

Carrie called my mom, who was picking me up at the airport, and asked her to share the results with me in person. When I landed, my mom met me at the baggage claim. "I have some bad news to tell you. You better sit down," she said.

"No, Mom, just tell me," I replied.

She shared that the MRI revealed a small growth at the base of Jackie's brain. I was saddened by the news but felt hopeful we could attack whatever the growth might be and remove it from her brain.

I turned right around and took the next plane back to Sacramento. By God's grace, a staff member from church, Dan, had been at Saddleback's preconference and just happened to be flying home to Sacramento on the same plane, so we ended up sitting together on the flight home.

The next day, Carrie and I met with the neurosurgeon, Dr. Pang, at the Kaiser in Sacramento. Dr. Pang examined Jackie in his office. Her reflexes seemed normal. He then asked his nurse to take Jackie into the waiting room for a few minutes. He showed us the x-ray from Jackie's MRI. He told us Jackie had a glioma brain stem tumor that was lodged at the base of her brain. The tumor was about two inches in circumference. The problem was it was enmeshed in her brain stem.

Dr. Pang told us that the tumor was so fast-growing and aggressive that it probably wasn't even in her brain three months earlier. It was a surreal moment. The irony was that while we were looking at the x-ray, Jackie was in the waiting room running the nurse ragged. She was so full of life. You couldn't tell from looking at her that anything was wrong.

While staring at the x-rays, I asked Dr. Pang, "What does this mean?"

"It means your daughter is going to die in the next two to three months," he replied.

We were in shock. I couldn't believe what we had just heard. I felt like I'd just been punched in the gut.

The bad news became even worse.

"Can you surgically remove the tumor?" I asked.

"I can't touch it," he replied.

"Why not?"

"I can't even biopsy it because it's enmeshed in her brainstem. We can't touch the brainstem because it's attached to the spinal cord," he explained.

"Is there anything we can do for her?" I asked.

"She's too young for chemotherapy. We can try radiation. It might shrink the tumor temporarily, but it will come back later with a vengeance and take her life," he replied.

I asked Dr. Pang how long he'd been a neurosurgeon? "Twenty years," he replied.

"In twenty years, have you ever seen someone with a tumor like this live an extended period of time?"

"No," he answered honestly.

As I tried to wrap my mind around the fact that Jackie was going to die within a couple of months, I had one final question to ask. "Will she suffer?" He didn't say a word. He just looked me at me and nodded yes.

At this point, I felt like I completely lost it. I couldn't bear the thought of my daughter dying in a few weeks, nor could I bear the thought of her suffering in the process.

"We're going to get a second opinion," I said.

"I would definitely get a second opinion if I were you," he replied. We agreed to see the radiologist and attempt radiation therapy.

Why God?

We left the hospital and stopped at a Sacramento restaurant for dinner. We went into the restaurant, and I started to fall apart. My eyes welled with tears, so I excused myself and returned to the car. I drove around the parking lot in the rain for twenty minutes. The thought of Jackie dying just didn't make any sense. Had I done something terribly wrong to deserve this? Had Carrie? "God, if I have, please forgive me," I prayed.

I was beside myself in pain. My heart was thumping. I was angry. I was angry at the Almighty. I pounded the steering wheel and screamed at God. "Why, God? Why her? Take me instead. This isn't fair," I screamed. I cried, yelled, and poured my heart out to God. I figured He could take it. I knew He didn't cause the tumor, but also knew He could have prevented it and He could heal her. But still, He allowed my daughter's tumor to form in her head.

I composed myself and returned to join my family in the restaurant. Carrie and Jackie were laughing together. "Jackie has something she would like to tell you," Carrie said.

"Daddy, I finally figured out how I'm going to stay a kid," Jackie giggled.

I Don't Want to Grow Up

Ever since Jackie was three years old, she never wanted to grow up; she always wanted to stay a kid. Most children when they are five years old want to be ten but Jackie was just the opposite.

A few months earlier, she was sprawled out on my lazy boy recliner. She had a grilled cheese sandwich in one hand, a glass of Sunny Delight in the other, and a SpongeBob cartoon on TV.

"Daddy, this is the life!" she said.

Jackie also never wanted to be a mother. I asked her once why that was the case, and she said, "Because a mommy's work is too hard." I laughed. She absolutely loved being a kid and didn't ever want to be anything else.

I played along, "So, you figured out how you're going to stay a kid?" I asked.

"Yes, I have," she replied.

"How are you going to do that? I asked.

"I'm going to die young," she replied. She said it with a smile on her face. I couldn't believe what I was hearing.

I glared at Carrie and asked, "What did you tell her?"

"I didn't tell her a thing. She came up with that all on her own," she explained.

God, in His mercy, was giving her glimpses of heaven and preparing her for her eternal home. He was also preparing us to let go.

When we got home, Carrie and I made a pact. We swore that no matter what happened, we were going to stay together. We were not going to separate or divorce. As a pastor, I knew the odds were against us. Most couples who have a child diagnosed with a terminal illness, or experience the death of a child, end up divorcing.

It's difficult because you want to seek comfort from your spouse, but they can't really comfort you because they're running on emotional fumes themselves. Our marriage was about to face the ultimate test.

The next day, Rick Warren, founding pastor of Saddleback Church, announced to a conference of three thousand pastors that my daughter was diagnosed with an inoperable brain stem tumor. Rick told me later that there was a hush throughout the crowd. There was a sense that this shouldn't happen to someone who had given his life to serve God. I think most pastors have this idea deep down but have never voiced it—that if we really love and serve Him, horrific things won't happen to us. I know I had this belief.

Rick called me that Friday night and asked if I wanted him to fly up to Auburn to be with us. He was willing to drop everything, including preaching at the weekend services at Saddleback, to keep us company. His offer meant the world to me, but I let him know we had family members on their way to see us that weekend.

He then offered to let me use any of his associate pastors to fill the pulpit at our church over the following few weeks, while I spent time with Jackie. I took him up on his offer as Lee Strobel, Doug Fields, and Tom Holladay flew up to speak in my absence. It was a real blessing for our church family. At that time, little did I know that several years later, Rick and Kay's youngest son, Matthew, would die from suicide.

After sharing the news with our family, Joshua, our nine-year-old son, pulled me aside and asked, "Dad, is Jackie going to die?"

I didn't know how to answer him. I didn't want to lie. I have always held to the belief that honesty with our children was crucial. "I don't know, son, but she could," I replied. My answer seemed to satisfy him at that moment.

In hopes of getting the second opinion we had sought after, we discovered that the top neurosurgeon in the world, Dr. Michael Edwards, the inventor of the Gamma Knife, had offices in Sacramento and San Francisco. The problem was he had a one-year waiting list to see patients. A couple of days later, his office called and said they had a cancellation and asked if we could be there in an hour. We met with Dr. Edwards, and he confirmed Dr. Pang's diagnosis. However, he informed us that no human being or doctor had a crystal ball that could accurately predict how much time a person would live. But in his opinion, he concurred with Dr. Pang's diagnosis and prognosis. Dr. Edwards felt Jackie had just weeks to months to live.

Radiation

We took Jackie to her first radiation appointment, and it turned out to be a horrible experience. The radiologist put Jackie in a room all by herself on a surgical table, had her lay on her stomach, and put a protection pad over her body to shield her from the radiation. Then, they closed the door, turned out the light, and pinpointed a bright red laser beam directly at the base of her brain. The process scared Jackie. She cried and tried to get off the table. They tried again and told her that she couldn't move in the process. After a few hours, they were finally able to complete a session that worked. Jackie was frightened the whole time and we were emotionally exhausted.

The radiologist prescribed daily treatments of radiation for six weeks. There was no way she could endure this procedure for that long. The radiation center suggested we have a Broviac catheter surgically put into Jackie and then sedate her each time to administer the radiation and then bring her out of the sedation. This seemed crazy to us but what other choice did we have?

Carrie and I prayed daily for wisdom. We prayed for God to show us what to do. I also prayed for strength each day. When my head hit my pillow at night, I thanked God for the strength he gave me that day. We decided to move forward with surgically installing the catheter in her chest to continue radiation treatment. Jackie had the brief surgery.

Carrie and I were with her in the recovery room when her eyes suddenly rolled to the back of her head and she stopped breathing. It looked like she was dying right then and there. "Code blue," the nurse yelled. Carrie ran out of the recovery room and into a hallway of the hospital. They were able to revive her within thirty seconds and she started breathing again and was crying.

I ran out to the hallway to get Carrie. She was curled up in a fetal position, her face entirely soaked in tears. "Is she dead? I knew she was going to die but I didn't think it would happen like this," she replied.

"No, she's okay. She's crying and wants to see you," I said. Carrie came back into the recovery room and held Jackie. We were so relieved.

The operating doctor took us aside and told us that it was our choice whether we wanted to continue with the daily radiation treatments. But he let us know that the growth of the tumor was already affecting her lungs, which had been compromised. He shared there was a good possibility that if we continued the radiation therapy, they may put her out and not be able to revive her.

We asked what other options we had. "Just one. Hospice," he replied. He shared that most kids five and under with inoperable brain tumors die in the hospital hooked up to tubes because their parents can't let go. We certainly didn't want Jackie to die that way. We were now facing the issue of quality-of-life versus quantity of life.

Hospice

We had prayed for God's guidance and felt hospice was our answer to prayer. Hospice workers are angels. They come to people for whom they care, at times of unique need, and stand ready to help however they can. We took Jackie home and put her on Hospice care so she could enjoy the final weeks of her life. We checked her out of the hospital, stopped at KB Toys on the way home, and told Jackie she could pick out any toy she wanted. She chose a beautiful stuffed animal.

While at the mall, we stopped to sit down. Jackie sat next to me, looked me squarely in the eyes, wrapped both hands around my neck, pulled my head in close to hers, and kissed me on the cheek without saying a word. She didn't need to. It was her way of saying, "Thank you, Daddy, for freeing me from the hospital."

Jackie came home and invited her girlfriends over for a tea party. Her friends couldn't tell anything was wrong with her.

Several people from church gave her stuffed animals as gifts. She lined up the stuffed animals against a wall in our family room. My associate pastor, Tim, stopped by to give Jackie another stuffed animal. "Welcome to Jackie's store! Pastor Tim, would you like to buy a stuffed animal?" she asked.

"How much are the stuffed animals, Ms. Jackie?" he played along.

"They are a dollar each," she replied. So, Tim picked out one he liked and invested a dollar into Jackie's new entrepreneurial business.

A few days later, my staff from church came over to our house to visit Jackie and pray with our family. They also brought a surprise for Jackie. My friend, Michael, worked for Wild Things, an exotic animal company that rented animals out for movies. Michael brought over a one-year-old chimpanzee. Jackie was scared at first but slowly warmed up to the monkey. At one point, the chimp did a backflip in the middle of our family room, then ran up my legs, onto my chest, and kissed me on the nose. The monkey scared me. Jackie laughed hysterically. The staff formed a circle around us and prayed for our family and for Jackie's healing.

The hospice nurse started coming on a regular basis to check on Jackie, take her vitals, and minister to her. This hospice nurse was a godsend. Jackie's stuffed animal store closed. Her tea parties stopped. Her little heart was slowing down in terms of beats per minute. She was sleeping a lot more and her body was beginning to shut down. Our hospice nurse said her time of passing was getting close, probably within days.

Janet, a neurological nurse and member of our church, asked us to call her when the time got close. I called her and she was at our house within ten minutes. Shortly thereafter, Jackie slipped into a coma. Janet was monitoring her heart and lungs. Her breathing got slower and slower, until it finally stopped. Her little lungs gave out.

In the next chapter of *The School of Grief* you will learn about death, facing a future you never dreamed possible and lasting hope.

CHAPTER 2:
THE DAY MY DAUGHTER DIED

> *"Yea, though I walk through the valley of the shadow of death, I will fear no evil: for thou art with me; thy rod and thy staff they comfort me"*
> *(Psalm 23:4 KJV).*

Jackie died peacefully in our arms on Saturday morning, March 4th.

I'd been dreading this day for weeks. In the agonizing last moments of her life and in the finality of her death, I felt the presence of God and a sense of peace even in the darkness and deep pain. Jackie died a peaceful death.

The neurosurgeon's prognosis that Jackie would suffer prior to her death never happened. She felt little to no pain in her last few weeks of life. No headaches, no vomiting, and no long-drawn-out death process. God was merciful as Jackie died just six weeks after her diagnosis. I'm thankful she never lost any cognitive ability, and she didn't die in a hospital hooked up to tubes. Rather, she passed away peacefully at our home.

Janet pronounced the time of death at 9:40 a.m. I cried harder than I'd ever cried in my life. I'd been expecting this moment since her diagnosis but when it came, it was overwhelming. I initially let out a loud wail followed by a torrent of tears. I could hear Carrie crying quietly beside me. My eyes were so drenched with sadness that everything was a blur. I was in shock. I thought my life had ended and in one sense, it had. Time stood still. Jackie looked so peaceful. She looked like she was sleeping. She couldn't be dead.

Words cannot express the pain and sorrow I felt at that moment. The day my daughter died was the worst day of my life. Nothing prepares a parent for such a moment. My anticipatory grief was mixed with hope that she may live longer than expected or may even survive this illness. I dreaded this moment would come. Now, it was here. The finality of the moment struck me. There's an awful finality to death. The party was over. The end. Her body was there but her spirit was gone.

I first started to grieve after her diagnosis and prognosis. I knew she had an inoperable brain tumor, and without divine intervention, I knew she would die. I tucked her into bed every night after her diagnosis and prayed with her, kissing her little head good night, knowing it may be my last kiss for my baby girl.

Jackie loved when I told her a particular story: "If I could line up all the little girls in the world, the line of little girls would extend around the earth. And if I could only pick one little girl out of the line as my favorite, I would pick you," I said. The biggest grin would grow on her face. "Why would

I pick you? Because you are my daughter. I love you and you make me happy," I added.

"Daddy, tell me that story again about all the little girls in the world," she replied. I have never told that story again.

I loved singing to Jackie. Jessica, her sister, would cover her ears to shield them from that awful noise that filled the car. I was singing my rendition of *You Are My Sunshine*: "You are my sunshine, my only sunshine. You make me happy when skies are gray. You'll never know dear, how much I love you. Please don't take my sunshine away."

I've always loved music, despite my apparent tone deafness. I would tap my fingers offbeat on the torn leather of the steering wheel while Jackie smiled like she was getting serenaded by Sinatra. She considered me to be a musical genius because she was under the impression that I had written this wonderful song. Whenever I told her otherwise, she thought I was just being modest and went on believing her dad was a rock star. Never in a million years would I have imagined that my sunshine would indeed be taken away from me.

I felt so bad for my wife. Carrie was a devoted mother who loved Jackie more than life itself. Jackie was a mommy's girl. All three kids were special, but Jackie was our baby. There is something special about the baby of the family. Carrie did everything for Jackie and Jackie loved her for it. I can't imagine how Carrie must have felt holding Jackie as she passed. This was the person who carried Jackie in her body for nine months, held her for the first time at birth, and who was now holding her limp body. Carrie would rock her to sleep. She loved her, kissed her, laughed with her, and cried with her. She would kiss her boo boo's and make them all better. It's just what moms do, and Carrie did it amazingly well. I am so proud that Carrie is the mother of my children.

Rituals like rocking her baby to sleep, breastfeeding her, changing her diapers, tucking her into bed, her first tooth, taking her first steps, learning how to swim, learning how to ride a bicycle, taking her to preschool, dance classes, and church, were all things she would never be able to do again in the coming weeks, months, and years.

Then, there were milestones that would never be realized—the secondary losses. Not being able to take her to school on her first day in first grade. Not celebrating her sweet sixteenth birthday, not attending her high school and college graduations, and not helping her get ready for prom. We would never be able to see Jackie grow up and become a woman, have children, and become a mother herself.

I cannot imagine how Jessica felt losing her little sister. Jackie idolized Jessica. She wanted to be just like her. They were only two years apart in age and shared a bedroom together, routinely staying up and talking themselves to sleep. Jessica dearly loved Jackie and was extremely patient, kind, and loving toward her. No child should have to lose a sibling at such a young age.

I cannot imagine how Joshua felt in losing his little sister, either. Joshua adored his baby sister. They were four years apart, so he didn't hang out with her, but Jackie made him laugh and he loved her dearly.

After Jackie died, Carrie asked me to go downstairs and let the kids know that their baby sister had gone to be with the Lord in heaven. How do you tell your kids that their sister is no longer with us? I went downstairs and found them on the couch playing video games.

"I have something I need to talk to you about," I said.

"Josh, turn off the video games," Jessica instructed.

"I'm so sorry to have to tell you that Jackie just died a few minutes ago." I saw tears welling up in their eyes.

"Daddy, what are we going to do now?" Jessica asked. As if she were saying, "All hope is gone; how will we survive?"

I thought for a moment and honestly didn't know what to say.

"I don't know, sweetie, but God will take care of us," I finally answered.

I think God gave me those words at that moment to assure my children that although tragedy had struck our family and although circumstances seemed out of control, we still had a heavenly Father who was in control and had a plan for our family. I invited them to come upstairs and say their own goodbyes to their sister.

Janet assured us we could wait a couple of hours before calling the coroner and mortuary. Carrie and her oldest sister, Sharon, gave Jackie a bath and dressed her in a beautiful dress. We took turns holding her.

Sweet Jackie looked angelic.

I called the coroner a couple of hours after our Jackie died. The coroner arrived first and confirmed and certified Jackie's death. He listed the immediate cause of death on her death certificate as cardiorespiratory arrest due to a glioma brain stem tumor. In other words, her little heart and lungs gave out.

A few minutes later, two men from the mortuary arrived to get Jackie. I picked up her little body. Rigor mortis had begun to set in. I carried her body with Carrie by my side, down to the van, and laid her inside. The van drove away with our baby. That moment was excruciating. I would later have nightmares every night about those men taking my daughter away. It was surreal. Here it was, a beautiful spring day in March. The sun was shining, the birds were singing, and the van was taking my daughter away.

Time went on. I wanted everything to stop. I wanted everybody to understand that my daughter had just died. But life went on.

Children are often the forgotten grievers. We all process grief in different ways, especially kids. Joshua had a basketball game that afternoon that he still wanted to play in. I told Carrie that I didn't think he should. She assured me it was okay for him to go play. "That's fine, but I'm not going," I said.

"But honey, you're the coach; you need to go," she insisted.

I went to the basketball game to support Joshua. During warm-ups, my assistant coach, Paul, asked, "How's Jackie doing?" People from church knew she was going to die soon but nobody knew that she had died that morning.

"Paul, Jackie died this morning at 9:40 a.m."

"She what? Oh my gosh, I didn't know. I'm so sorry," said Paul.

"I know, it came even sooner than we thought. She slipped into a coma and passed quickly," I said.

"What are you doing here?" Paul asked.

"I came for Joshua. You're going to have to coach today because I'm not able," I said.

The next hour was a blur as I watched my son run up and down the court. After the game was over, we went home. Joshua went back to playing video games. We all deal with our emotions in different ways.

The next day was Sunday. Carrie's parents had spent the night with us. Carrie was up early making breakfast. I woke up at 7:00 a.m. I realized when I awoke that Jackie was no longer with us. Not just no longer with us in spirit, but no longer physically with us in our home.

Around 10:00 a.m., I had a strong feeling that I wanted to go to see our church family and personally invite them to Jackie's funeral that would be held on Saturday. We had three Sunday morning services, two had already passed, but one was left at 11:00 a.m. I asked Carrie, Joshua, and Jessica if they wanted to go with me. Carrie and Joshua declined, but Jessica accepted and came along.

I got up on stage, sat down on a stool, and shared about my daughter's death, inviting all of them to her funeral service. I broke down while sharing and expressed my heartfelt love for each of them as our spiritual family.

No Words

When you lose a child, you join a fraternity or sorority you didn't want to join: parents who have lost a child. When someone loses a spouse, they are called a *widow* or *widower*. When a child loses a parent, he or she is called an *orphan*. But there are no words in the English language to describe a parent who loses a child. Why? I think there are two reasons: First, it's commonly assumed that parents will outlive their children. Second, the grief associated with losing a child is so horrific that no word could possibly do it justice in describing the excruciating pain associated with such an experience.

Prior to my daughter's death, I looked forward to the future. Now, I was facing a future I hadn't planned and didn't want. I couldn't see a future for myself beyond my pain. My future seemed as dim as the thick tule fog that settles in the Sacramento Valley each fall.

We have a difficult time imagining a future without our loved one. We continue to picture what our life would have been and yearn for that preferred future. It's a future that is no longer possible, but we still strongly desire it. It's easier to remember the past with our loved one than it is to imagine a future without them.

In the next chapter of *The School of Grief,* you will learn whether your life can be good again after your loss.

CHAPTER 3:
WILL LIFE EVER BE GOOD AGAIN?

> *"Birds sing after a storm; why shouldn't people feel as free to delight in whatever sunlight remains to them?"*
> Rose Fitzgerald Kennedy

Jerry Sittser, a religion professor, and author of *A Grace Disguised*, was involved in a terrible auto accident. A drunk driver hit his minivan, killing Jerry's mother, wife, and four year old daughter—three generations at once. Jerry survived, along with his three other children who had significant injuries. When I read his story, I felt I'd been punched in the gut again.

The book gives Jerry's reflections on the tragedy and its effect on his faith. After writing this best-selling book, he received thousands of letters and emails from readers around the world. One question kept surfacing. Surprisingly, it wasn't a theological question but a human, practical and gut-wrenching one: *Will my life ever be good again?*[1]

THE SCHOOL OF GRIEF

You probably want to know if life has any joy in store for you in your future after your loss. I wondered the exact same thing immediately after losing Jackie. In fact, this became my number one question and concern.

Catastrophic loss is so overwhelming and its consequences so far-reaching that it seems improbable that we will ever experience goodness again. When you equate goodness with what you once had, you will be sorely disappointed. Loss is irreversible. Life will never be the same. Your life as you knew it before is over. Loss brings with it a whole new life change.

I needed hope to survive and assurance that my life could be good again in the future. Maybe you are searching for hope as well after your loss. I honestly didn't know how to process my grief, what to do, or where to turn.

Out of desperation, I called Dr. Sittser at Whitworth University, and asked if he would come speak at the church I pastored in Auburn. It was totally for selfish reasons: to help me deal with my grief. We talked on the phone for ten minutes, and he informed me that he had a year waiting list for speaking engagements. I thanked him for his time, and we were ready to end the call when he asked, "How long ago did your daughter die?"

"Two weeks ago," I replied.

"Two weeks ago. I thought it was a year or two ago!" he exclaimed. Jerry told me he would talk with his kids and if they were okay with him coming, he would join me in a couple of weeks.

Jerry flew from Spokane to Auburn and taught at each of our weekend services at church. His message was called, *How to Survive Suffering.* I hung onto every word he said. He shared about how God brings joy through suffering. Sunday afternoon, he spoke with our small groups leaders about launching grief support groups at our church.

I spent time with Jerry as he helped me frame my loss. He became a role model of someone who had suffered great loss and yet had joy in his life. It surprised me that a man could suffer such devastation and yet still love God, his family (what remained), other people, and life. He had a smile on his face and a bounce in his step. I wanted to be like Jerry. I figured if he could do it, then maybe I could, too. And maybe you can, as well.

Author and poet, Helen Steiner Rice, wrote, "Comfort comes from knowing that people have made the same journey. And solace comes from understanding how others have learned to sing again."

Jerry had learned to sing again after his loss. I thought if God could transform Jerry, maybe He could transform me, too. It seemed totally impossible at the time, but Jesus once said, "With God all things are possible" (Matthew 19:26).

Hope

We all need hope to cope with our loss. Author Seth Godin said, "Hope is an essential part of the human condition. Without hope we wither and perish." Hope for the bereaved is like oxygen for a deep-sea diver; without it, you die inside. You can survive forty days without food, three days without water, and eight minutes without air. But you can't last a single second without hope. It's an essential part of life. When hope is gone, life is over.

We all need hope mentors, people who have walked the journey of grief, gone where we want to go, and are willing to teach us what they learned along the way. Jerry Sittser was evidence to me of someone who had hope after loss. I sought to learn everything I could from him.

Author David Kessler said, "A loved one's death is permanent, and that is so heartbreaking. But I believe your loss of hope can be temporary. Until you can find it, I'll hold hope for you. I have hope for you. Death ends a life, but not our relationship, not our love, or our hope." [2]

I hold hope for people who have lost it, as well. Your loved one's death on earth is permanent but considering eternity, it's just temporary. The good news is that Jesus overcame death by rising from the dead and he promises us new life together with him in heaven where there is no more death, mourning, or pain. Nothing, including death, can separate us from the love of God.

I believe there is only one place to find real and lasting hope and that is by turning to God: "May God, the source of hope, fill you with joy and peace through your faith in him. Then you will overflow with hope by the power of the Holy Spirit" (Romans 15:13 GW).

Life Will Never be the Same but Life Can be Good Again

I will never recover from my loss, and I will never get over missing Jackie. I will always want what I lost back. We recover from broken limbs but not from amputations. Losing my daughter felt like a piece of my life had been cut off. We can't go back to the past but we can create a new future. Recovering what we had before is not possible but healing and growth are. I will always have an emotional scar on my heart with Jackie's name on it.

Grief never ends on this earth. There is no expiration date. Many people struggle with this idea of grieving forever—I know I did. At first, I just wanted my grief to end. I craved for the pain to stop. I desired to go from heartbreak to happiness in one year or less, but it doesn't work that way.

Psychiatrist and author, Elizabeth Kübler Ross, wrote, "The reality is that you will grieve forever. You will not *get over* the loss of a loved one; you will learn to live with it. You will heal and rebuild yourself around the loss you have suffered. You will be whole again, but you will never be the same. Nor should you be the same!"[3]

Being human brings heartache. Healing from our heartache is a slow process. We need to not think about grief as something with an end destination, but rather as an ongoing healing journey.

I've walked this journey now for two decades and will continue to embrace an ongoing connection with my daughter. I wouldn't want it any other way. My grief for her will never end because my love for her will never end.

I am who I am today because of my daughter's life and death. These two realities will always be a part of my story. The good news is that grief does get easier over time, less painful. You find that there are ways to cope with the pain and that healing comes through God and through community.

I discovered my life would never be the same again after my loss. I don't want it to be the same. I've changed. I've grown. I'm not the same person I was before my loss. But I've also found life can be surprisingly good again. Life is different now but very meaningful and satisfying. I enjoy my life but in an altered way—a more grateful, humble, and compassionate way.

I have a new relationship with my daughter as I carry the gift of her life, impact, and memory with me forever. I have a renewed faith and newfound optimism. I've found hope, meaning, and purpose through my pain and am excited to share it with you.

One reason I wrote this book is so you might find hope after your loss. I'll hold hope for you temporarily and pray that you experience the grace of God and find hope for yourself.

In the next chapter of *The School of Grief*, I will provide an overview of grief. You will learn the difference between grief and mourning, how to grieve with hope, a helpful timeline, and why the grief process is like peeling an onion.

PART TWO:
UNDERSTANDING GRIEF

CHAPTER 4:
WHAT IS GRIEF?

> *"Grief is like the ocean; it comes on waves ebbing and flowing. Sometimes the water is calm, and sometimes it is overwhelming. All we can do is learn to swim."*
> ***Vicki Harrison***

What is Grief?

Grief is brutal and intensely personal. It's a universal experience that we, as human beings, inevitably face because death is the ultimate disrupter of life. Grief is a natural response to any loss. It's an intense emotion we experience after a significant loss, like the death of a loved one, a divorce, the loss of a pet or job, or a terminal illness diagnosis. Grief is a multifaceted sensory experience that typically manifests itself in physical pain, feelings of numbness, hopelessness, loneliness, and deep sorrow.

In a word, Grief is *change*. Mark Twain said, "The only person who likes change is a baby with a wet diaper." Loss brings changes into our lives, usually ones we didn't want. Grief is the recognition of that change, but it's also the loss of a connection. At its core, grief is *love*; it's love for whatever we had that is now gone.

One morning, Sheryl Sandberg, the former COO of Facebook and the mother of two kids, found her husband, Dave, collapsed on the floor of their home gym. He never woke again. She was devastated.

Two weeks later, Sheryl was talking to her friend, Phil, about a father-child activity. They came up with a plan for someone to fill in for Dave. Sheryl cried out to Phil, "But I want Dave."

Her friend put his arm around Sheryl and said, "Option A is not available. So, let's just kick the shit out of Option B."[1] Racy language. Wise counsel.

Life is never perfect. Sooner or later, we all lose Option A in our lives. Navigating the grief journey is learning how to live and thrive with Option B.

The Weight of Grief

Grief is weight. The word comes from the Middle English *gref* and the Latin *gravis*, both words meaning heavy.[2] A common adjective people use in speaking of grief is *unbearable*. Grief is a burden you bear, a heavy weight you learn to carry.

Please give yourself permission to grieve. You have that right. Don't ever let someone take your grief away from you. You give yourself permission to grieve by recognizing your need to do so. Grieving is not weakness nor is it the absence of faith; it is as natural as crying when you're sad, yawning when you're bored, or sleeping when you're tired. Grieving is God's way of healing your broken heart.

Don't Compare Your Grief

There's a natural tendency to compare our loss and grief with others. Don't play the grief-comparison game. The problem is if you win, you lose. Comparing grief merely based on the type of loss is a mistake that leaves people feeling *less than* and not deserving of the same kind of support. There is no hierarchy of grief, with some loss perceived as being *worse* than others. All grief is important. One person's grief doesn't need to be worse than someone else's for it to be significant. The worst kind of loss is your loss.

What you think of someone else's loss and grief is none of your business. Jesus told Peter to mind his own business when Peter asked how John would die. Peter asked, "Lord, what about him?" Jesus answered, "What I have planned for John isn't any of your business. What is that to you? You follow me" (John 21:21).

Timeline for Grief

I always begin by asking someone in grief when their loss happened. This helps me assess where they are on the timeline provided below. While we know there is no timeline for grief because no two people experience grief the same way, the simple timeline below can help us gauge necessary interventions.

For example, if I'm counseling someone who shares they are driving a mile out of their way to work each day because they are triggered by the radiation center where their loved one had a bad experience, I would encourage them to take the mile detour to take care of themselves initially. However, if they are stilling driving the detour three years later, I might suggest that it's time to face that fear. There are four types of grief outlined below:

- Anticipatory grief - Grief that comes before the death or loss.
- Acute grief: Grief right after the death or loss occurs.
- Early grief: The first two years of grief.
- Mature grief: Grief for the rest of our lives.[3]

What's the Distinction Between Grief and Grieving?

Mary-Frances O'Connor, author of *The Grieving Brain*, makes a distinction between *grief* and *grieving*.[4] Grief is that overwhelming emotion that comes over us like a wave after our loss. The feeling is so intense that we want to know when it will be over. If you think the waves of grief will stop at some point, you will be sadly disappointed and think something is wrong with you when they don't. The waves will decrease in frequency and intensity over time, but they will never completely go away.

Grieving, on the other hand, is the process of change that occurs after our loss. We are faced with a problem when we lose someone or something dear to us. We now need to figure out how to live in a world without that someone or something. Grieving is a form of learning; that's why I titled this book, "The School of Grief." It's learning how to carry the absence of our loved one with us and learning how to navigate our new existence on earth. Grieving is our way of processing, changing, adapting, and working through our loss of love. Through the grieving process, we slowly learn how to comfort ourselves in our pain. As we become more familiar with the waves, we learn how to better deal with them, and even how to ride some of them.

What's the Difference Between Grief and Mourning?

Grief is what's going on inside us, while mourning is what we do on the outside. The internal work of grief is ongoing, that's why I refer to it as our grief journey. Mourning, on the other hand, is an outward sign of our grief. In relation to this, Jesus said, "Blessed are those who mourn" (Matthew 5:4). The present tense indicates that the mourning is continual. He doesn't say, "Blessed are those who mourned." The reality is there is no timeline for grief and no cure. We carry our loss in our hearts for the rest of our lives. Jesus promises us comfort as we mourn. He doesn't promise to take away all our pain, but he does promise us solace.

Bereaved

A bereaved person is one who has a relative or close friend who has recently died. The Old English word *bereave* means *to rob*. The word implies we've been robbed or stripped of someone or something, often suddenly and unexpectedly, and sometimes by force. I concur with this definition. I felt like I was I robbed when I lost my daughter to a brain tumor, like she was snatched out of my life. It was as if cancer took her life by force and there was nothing I could do. My daughter's life on earth was robbed from me and my future with her was ripped apart.

Rending a Garment in Grief

In biblical times, it was common for Jews to mourn by tearing their clothes. It's natural to feel anger when someone or something is snatched out of your life. Rending one's garments was a tangible expression of grief and anger in the face of death. For example, David tore his clothes when Saul and his beloved friend, Jonathan, were killed.

Why? Because in an agrarian society, clothing was a very valuable commodity. Nothing was mass-produced. Clothes were time-intensive and expensive, so most people at that time had a very limited wardrobe. People who tore their clothes were displaying how upset they felt internally. By damaging one of their more important and expensive possessions, it reflected the depth of their emotional pain. This idea was magnified when people chose to put on *sackcloth* after tearing clothes. Sackcloth was a coarse and scratchy material and was extremely uncomfortable. As with tearing their garments, people put on sackcloth to externally display the discomfort and pain they felt inside.

Psalms of Lament

A lament is a passionate expression of our sorrow and regret to God. It's an act of worship that includes crying out to God, yelling, complaining, even arguing with the Almighty. God isn't afraid of our negative emotions. In fact, there's an entire book of lament in the Bible called Lamentations, where Jeremiah complains to God about his life. Nearly fifty percent of the Book of Psalms are psalms of lament. God wants us to express our feelings and get it off our chest.

There are two types of lament psalms: communal and individual. Communal laments deal with situations of national crisis. For instance, David orders the people to join him in singing a lamentation he wrote: "O daughters of Israel, weep for Saul" (2 Sam 1:24 NKJV). David asks others to join him in pouring out their grief and tears for King Saul after he died.

Individual laments deal with problems faced by one member of the people of God. For instance, David wrote: "Why, Lord, do you stand far off? Why do you hide yourself in times of trouble?" (Psalm 10:1). David wonders why the wicked prosper while God seemingly stands aloof and detached as he and others suffer.

It's tempting when we are suffering to look around and compare ourselves and our grief to others. We don't yet see the full picture and wonder why God appears not to care about us. As if the Psalmist is saying, "Pay attention to me, God, help me out here!" I know God isn't a distant Deity and he does hear my cries and responds. But sometimes in my pain, I get upset and impatient when God doesn't seem to be responding according to my time frame.

Grieving with Hope

We will all grieve at some point in life, but believers grieve slightly differently from the world because we can maintain hope even in our deepest times of sorrow. The Bible affirms the importance of grief and instructs Christians how to grieve. The Apostle Paul tells us believers will grieve and have their share of trials, tragedies, and difficult losses. You don't get excused because you are a follower of Jesus.

Paul says, "We want you to know what will happen to the believers who have died so you will not grieve like people who have no hope. For since we believe that Jesus died and was raised to life again, we also believe that when Jesus returns, God will bring back with him the believers who have died ...

So, encourage each other with these words" (1 Thessalonians 4:13-14,18 NLT).

We often think of death as a departure, but for believers in Christ, it's, in fact, an arrival. Death is the doorway by which you can leave the limitations and pains of this world to enter the heavenly realm and be given the gift of eternal life. The grave is an entrance into new life. It's a door, not a wall. Death is not saying a last "goodbye" but rather saying, "See you later." We grieve differently, yet honestly and openly, because we look forward to going to heaven, seeing Jesus, and being reunited with our loved ones who have gone before us.

Death isn't the worst thing that can happen to us; rather, for believers, death leads to the best possible scenario. Paul said, "For to me, to live is Christ and to die is gain… I desire to depart and be with Christ, which is better by far" (Philippians 1:21,23).

Therefore, we grieve with hope. Our hope doesn't nullify our grief; rather, hope puts grief into an eternal context. I'm not saying non-believers can't grieve fully and find hope again after their loss. My point is that believers are called to grieve differently. The biblical approach to grieving is a hopeful approach. It's hope in the person, resurrection, and love of Christ that allows us to find comfort even in our pain.

Grief is Like Peeling an Onion

My favorite illustration for understanding grief comes from Doug Manning, a former pastor turned grief expert who I had the privilege of working under in learning how to perform memorial services. He describes grief as being a lot like peeling an onion. It comes off one layer at a time and you cry a lot. Just like there is no right or wrong way to grieve, there is no right way to peel away the layers.[5]

The days between a death and the funeral service are like the paper-thin outer skin of an onion that comes off easily and blows away in the wind. That's when the bereaved person is in shock and is surrounded by family and friends trying to bring comfort.

The funeral is often the climactic event in the care of the family as the bereaved have their grief witnessed. Once that superficial outer skin is removed, then the real grieving process begins in three identifiable layers: reality, reaction, and reconstruction.

1. Reality

If you take the thin outer skin of an onion, crumble it up and toss it up into the wind, it's a good picture of the initial shock of grief. It is a period of confusion and a denial of reality as everything is in a whirl. A few weeks after the funeral, the shock wears off and the reality of the loss sets in. That's when some people break down.

2. Reaction

At some point, anger will emerge. Anger is a secondary emotion that we bolt over to when we've been hurt. When the anger surfaces, it means the bereaved is starting to fight back. Anger needs a place to focus. The object of anger may be the deceased person, a doctor, a pastor, a family member, or even God. I got extremely angry at God when my daughter died, even though I knew He didn't cause her cancer. But at that time, I believed He could have cured it and chose not to. Anger is a healthy emotion in grief. I'd be concerned for you if you weren't angry after experiencing a significant loss. It only becomes unhealthy when it becomes internalized and self-directed.

3. Reconstruction

Grief is traumatic but can also be transformative. Eventually, the grieving person will start to progress on their grief journey and begin to reconstruct their life. At this point, the griever needs a companion to walk alongside them, to listen to their anger and help them realize that life will never be like it was before the loss. The pain that comes from grief is cruel but be assured that the sharp pain will eventually become a dull ache.

If I gave each person who reads this book an onion, no two people would have an onion alike. Onions come in different sizes, shapes, and colors, mirroring the ways in which the dimensions of grief are very different. Manning suggests four dimensions of grief: significance, lonely, delayed, and shattered.[6]

Significance Dimension (Loss of a Child)

The grief following the death of a child has a *significance dimension*. Grief after losing a child is a process of hanging on and trying to not say goodbye because you don't feel like the child has lived long enough to establish their significance.

Lonely Dimension (Miscarriage and Stillbirth)

Grief following miscarriage or stillbirth has a *lonely dimension* because the mother is the only one who really knows that child. She bonded with them from the moment of conception. The father may have a connection with the child because he felt them kicking in the womb, but the mother really *knows* that child. Her grief then becomes an issue of explaining the value of that life to a world that thinks that stillbirth is minor grief.

Delayed Dimension (Murder)

Murder or sudden death has a *delayed dimension*. This is especially true for murder because until they catch the person, have the trial (which is usually a painful experience for the family), and experience a verdict, the grief is on hold. With other kinds of sudden death, the shock is so deep that it takes a while before loved ones can begin to deal with the grieving process.

Shattered Dimension (Suicide)

Suicide has a *shattered dimension*. You feel like the onion has just been blown apart, and you must put it back together before you can peel it. Families will often search for who said what, what was done, and who caused it. Manning once said, "'Twas the final straw that broke the camel's back, then men noticed the fiendish pack, but who among them saw the next to the last straw."[7]

Suicide is the culmination of a complex package, a combination of all kinds of straws that one day became overwhelming. It's not ever just the last straw that is to blame.

One of the difficulties with grieving suicide loss is that everybody feels guilty. We think we should have known and should have been able to stop it. Neither of those is true. The only one who could have stopped the suicide is the one who died of suicide. Suicide victims often seem better just before the suicide; therefore, it is very difficult to detect.

Sudden death and death by suicide can complicate the grieving process because they are so traumatic and because the family and friends didn't get a chance for closure.

Grief Can Feel Like Being Crushed by a Boulder

Grieving is hard work; some of the hardest work I've ever done in my life is mourning my losses. Metaphors for grief help us find language to express how we are feeling. Finding words helps us make some sense of our losses.

Kay Warren shared with a group of grieving women that the loss of her son felt like a gigantic boulder that fell from the sky and crushed her to the ground, completely devastating her. Kathy, a close friend, shared with Kay that someday, that boulder would become the size of a rock she could hold in her pocket and carry with her. It will never go away entirely, but it won't always feel like it's crushing her.

Ocean Waves of Grief

I grew up in Southern California and one of my favorite activities was going to the beach. When I was a kid, my parents owned an apartment complex in Laguna Beach that we often frequented and it was there I learned about the ocean, waves, boogie boarding, surfing, and grief.

After my daughter died, I felt like I was drowning in grief. It was hard to breathe. Going through the grief process is like being caught in a set of big waves. Waves of anger, doubt, denial, sadness, depression, helplessness, and confusion kept crashing down on me. Maybe you feel like that right now.

Despite what some experts say, the grief process is not a neat and tidy set of stages you successfully go through and move on from. Instead, grief comes in emotional waves that come in different sizes and shapes, knocking the hell out of you. Grief is overwhelming.

I remember bodysurfing one time when a set of waves came out of nowhere and trapped me. I was thrust underwater for what seemed like an eternity but was only a few seconds. I just wanted to breathe. I tried to let the air pour into my lungs. When I surfaced, I found another huge wave bearing down on me and under I went.

When the wave breaks, you're broadsided, and you find yourself tossing, spinning, and bouncing off the bottom of the ocean with a mouth full of salt water and sand. If you fight, it takes longer to get to the surface. But if you float with the current (your body is buoyant), you will rise to the top. Floating when we are frightened is difficult. Dealing with death and the grief that follows is similar.

Going to the beach has taught me to respect the ocean and its power. Water is one of the most powerful forces on earth, so is grief. You never want to turn your back on the ocean. I remember when my mom and I were walking on some rocks at Laguna looking at starfish. We turned our backs on the ocean for just a few seconds to walk back to shore when a big wave came out of nowhere and knocked us off our feet, dragging us across the rocks. We emerged bloody and bruised but learned an important lesson. Turning your back on the ocean is like turning your back on grief and ignoring it; it will hurt you.

When a woman on Reddit was mourning the loss of her best friend and seeking support by chatting with strangers, a commenter, who called himself *old man*, wrote a piece that

WHAT IS GRIEF?

went viral about how grief comes in waves. Here is an excerpt from what he wrote:

"In the beginning, the waves are 100 feet tall and crash over you without mercy. They come 10 seconds apart and don't even give you time to catch your breath. All you can do is hang on and float. After a while, maybe weeks, maybe months, you'll find the waves are still 100 feet tall, but they come further apart. When they come, they still crash all over you and wipe you out. But in between, you can breathe, you can function. You never know what's going to trigger the grief. It might be a song, a picture, a street intersection, the smell of a cup of coffee. It can be just about anything…and the wave comes crashing. But in between waves, there is life.

"Somewhere down the line, and it's different for everybody, you find that the waves are only 80 feet tall. Or 50 feet tall. And while they still come, they come further apart. You can see them coming. An anniversary, a birthday, or Christmas, or landing at O'Hare. You can see it coming, for the most part, and prepare yourself. And when it washes over you, you know that somehow you will, again, come out the other side. Soaking wet, sputtering …but you'll come out.

"Take it from an old guy. The waves never stop coming, and somehow you don't really want them to. But you learn that you'll survive them. And other waves will come. And you'll survive them too. If you're lucky, you'll have lots of scars from lots of loves."[8]

The waves won't stop coming but you can survive the waves. God will help you breathe and will make a way for you. You'll gain confidence along the way and discover that grief will not take you down. You will survive. Remember, your life will never be the same; it will be different. But sometimes, different can be okay, too.

In the next chapter of *The School of Grief*, you will learn three helpful models of grief. Grief models help us better understand what to expect in our grief journey. They reveal common emotions that may surprise and overwhelm us with their intensity as we work our way through the grieving process.

CHAPTER 5:
MODELS OF GRIEF

> *"The five stages of grief were never meant to tuck messy emotions into neat packages."*
> **Elisabeth Kübler-Ross**

Grief is Messy

Grief is a tangled ball of emotions. It's messy, traumatic, confusing, and overwhelming. It can make you feel like you're going crazy. Grief can make you question your faith. It doesn't color within the lines. Your emotions may be all over the place but that's normal. The diagram below illustrates how we want grief to work and how it actually works.

How we <u>want</u> grief to work	How grief <u>actually</u> works

61

Models of grief are guidelines of what people may experience when grieving. However, if you do not fit a model, it does not mean there is something wrong with the way you experience grief. There is no one way to grieve, and people move through a variety of stages of grief in various ways. The stages aren't meant to tuck messy emotions into a neat package but are responses to loss that many people have, yet there is no typical response to loss because there is no typical loss. Below are three models of grief to help you better understand your grief.

Elisabeth Kübler Ross: Five Stages of Grief

Dr. Ross describes five emotional stages people pass through on their grief journey: denial, anger, bargaining, depression, and acceptance. These stages, and the ease of remembering them through the acronym DABDA, have become part of our popular culture. Dr. Ross first identified the stages of dying in her book, *On Death and Dying*, as stages people passed through prior to death and later applied them to be stages of grief.[1]

Denial helps us survive the loss. In this stage, the world becomes overwhelming and meaningless. Life doesn't make sense. We are emotionally numb and wonder how we can ever go on—or why we should go on at all. Denial helps us get through the day, helps us cope, and makes survival possible.

Anger is an important and necessary stage of the healing process. Allow yourself to feel your anger although it may seem limitless. The more you feel it, the more it will dissipate and the more you will heal. You may ask, "Where is God in my loss?" I have a friend named Dennis who lost his wife to a sudden death. He did the eulogy at her memorial and began by asking, "What the hell, God?" I told him after the service how proud I was that he was voicing his anger. Underneath his anger was pain. It's natural to feel deserted or abandoned after a loss, but we live in a society that fears anger. Your anger is an indication of the intensity of your love.

Bargaining is that stage where you find yourself negotiating with yourself, with people around you, with fate, or even with God to try to change or undo your loss. Before Jackie died, I begged God to take me and not her. After she died, I would have given anything to bring her back. We want life to return to normal; we want our loved one restored.

Depression is not a sign of mental illness. It is a natural response to a great loss and a part of the grieving process. When the loss fully settles into your soul, the realization that your loved one isn't coming back is depressing. Depression is one of the necessary steps toward healing.

Acceptance is confused with being all right with what has happened. This is not the case. I have never felt okay about losing Jackie. This stage is about accepting the reality that my daughter is physically gone and that this is my new permanent reality on this earth. I will never like this reality, but I have learned to accept it and live with the fact that I now live in a world where my daughter is missing.

David Kessler worked with Dr. Ross and saw the need to add a sixth stage to her five-stage model. He wrote a book called, *Finding Meaning: The Sixth Stage of Grief*. After Kessler lost his son, he felt he couldn't stop with the fifth stage of acceptance. It wasn't enough. He wanted more. He wanted to find meaning from his son's loss.

Meaning is a way to keep your loved one's memory alive and to honor them. It's finding the part of them that lives in you and taking it into your new future. Or, if they died tragically, it's searching for a way to change the world so other people don't die the same way.

Finding meaning after loss is deeply personal, something you define for yourself, and can look very different for each person. If you have found meaning after your loss, I am thrilled for you. And if you're still in the process, please don't give up hope.

Rick Warren: Six Stages of Grief

Rick Warren is my mentor, friend, and hero. I met him three decades ago and he trained me as a pastor and church planter. He believed in me as a young man, and I'm forever grateful. Like me, Rick is a grieving pastor and dad. He has an amazing ability to teach profound concepts in a simple way, which he does with grief.

Sixteen weeks after his son's death, Rick taught a series called, *Getting Through What You're Going Through*. In the series, he identifies six stages of reaction to loss: shock, sorrow, struggle, surrender, sanctification, and service.[2]

Shock is experienced when your world falls apart. Rick's son, Matthew, dealt with mental health issues, but it was still a huge shock to the Warren family when he died from suicide. For the first month, Rick was waiting for Matthew to walk through the door.

Sorrow is experienced when your heart breaks because of your loss. It's a feeling of profound sadness. But sorrow is also a godly emotion. The only reason we're able to grieve is because we're made in the image of God. Jesus was a man acquainted with sorrow. Grieving is healthy. It's the way God designed for us to respond to life's transitions.

Struggle is the stage you experience when you don't understand. Nothing seems to make sense. It's where you ask the *why* questions: Why me? Why now? Why did this happen? Some people will tell you that *why* is not a good question. I disagree. I think it's a great question and I still ask it. You're probably not going to get answers to your *why*, but it's still okay to ask. Even Jesus asked *why* on the cross when he said, "My God! My God! Why...?" Life is a struggle, and the real test of your faith is what you do when you don't get the answer because most likely, you won't.

After Matthew died, Warren wrote in his journal, "I'd rather walk with God with none of my questions answered than walk through life without him and know all the answers." Even if you did get an explanation, it's not going to bring comfort from the pain. What you need in a time of tragedy is not an explanation but the presence and love of God.

Surrender is the stage where you stop asking, start surrendering, and begin to accept your loss. Surrender is the path to peace. Rick said, "I'd rather have all my questions unanswered and walk with God than not walk with God and have all my questions answered. I never questioned my faith in God, but I questioned God's plan." Not everything that happens in this world is God's will. God permits it but we live in a world where we have choices. Even after his loss, Rick continued to affirm God's goodness and doesn't blame God for his son's death.

Sanctification is the stage where your life begins to change. There is no growth without change. There is no change without loss. There is no loss without grief. There is no grief without pain. The pain of our loss can motivate us to change. Loss can be traumatic, but it can also be transformative. Sanctification is the change process we go through like the metamorphosis of a caterpillar into a butterfly. Over time, we can become better because of our loss rather than bitter. We can become more compassionate and empathetic human beings.

Service is the final stage. It deals with using your pain for good, rather than wasting your hurt. It's realizing that God wants to use your hurt and pain to help others. Who can better help parents of a child with Down Syndrome than parents who have had a child with Down Syndrome?

J. William Worden: Four Tasks of Grief

In his book, *Grief Counseling and Grief Therapy*, Psychologist J. William Worden provides a framework of four tasks that help us understand how we journey through grief. Healing happens gradually as grievers address these tasks, in no particular order, going back and forth from one to another over time. Worden suggests that the following four tasks must be accomplished for the process of mourning to be completed and for equilibrium to be reestablished.[3]

Task 1: To Accept the Reality of the Loss

Although you know on an intellectual level that the person has died, you may still be in shock and not believe it. For example, the reality may begin to set in when you must call the mortuary, attend the funeral, or pick up the ashes.

A common struggle with this task in around acceptance of the means of the death. A death by suicide, overdose, or other sudden death can present challenges to accomplishing this task if family and friends don't acknowledge or accept the reality of how the loved one died.

Task 2: To Process the Pain of Grief

Grief is experienced emotionally, cognitively, physically, and spiritually. You must experience the pain of what you have lost in your mind, body, and soul. Allow the emotion into your consciousness and begin to take steps to process your feelings. Rather than trying to identify all the emotions of grief, Worden affirms that every person is unique and experiences a range of different emotions. This process takes time and differs depending on the individual.

Task 3: To Adjust to a World Without the Deceased

This task deals with adjusting to the environment in which the deceased is missing. Worden acknowledges this task is different for everyone, depending on the relationship with the person who died, and the roles that are affected by the loss. This readjustment involves internal, external, and spiritual adjustments. Internal adjustments are made as you adapt to your new identity without your loved one. External adjustments include trying to learn new skills and taking on new responsibilities. Spiritual adjustments happen as you wrestle with questions about your beliefs and the meaning and purpose of your new life without your loved one.

Task 4: To Find an Enduring Connection with the Deceased While Embarking on a New Life

Gradually, you create a balance between remembering the person who died and living a full and meaningful life. For some people, life stopped when their loved one died and they were no longer able to resume their life in a meaningful way.

They could not figure out how to establish a different sense of connection to their loved one who has died. This last task takes time and can be one of the most difficult to accomplish. Worden feels mourning is successfully accomplished when a person has completed all four tasks.

Over the years, Worden has improved upon his four tasks. He is continually re-evaluating and refining his own theory. As the world's understanding of grief grows, Worden is committed to updating his tasks to reflect this new and developing understanding.

In the next chapter of *The School of Grief*, you will learn the best and worst things to say to those in grief, including tips for talking to grieving people, and how to respond to people in pain.

CHAPTER 6:
THE BEST AND WORST THINGS TO SAY

> *"Never tell someone in grief to get over it or move on. People experience grief in their own way and in their own time. We live in a fix-it society. There is nothing to fix because they are not broken."*
> *David Kessler*

Don't Tell Me to Move On

In today's world, we often share our grief feelings on social media. Kay Warren is the co-founder of Saddleback Church, a mental health advocate, and dear friend. She was angry at what some people had said to her in her grief. She had a right to be angry. Her son, Matthew, died from suicide. Here is part of a Facebook post she wrote titled, *Don't Tell Me to Move On*:[1]

"As the one year anniversary of Matthew's death approaches, I have been shocked by some subtle and not-so-subtle comments indicating that perhaps I should be ready to *move on*... I have to tell you – the old Rick and Kay are gone. They're never coming back. We will never be the same again.

"Because these comments from well-meaning folks wounded me so deeply, I doubted myself and thought perhaps I really am not grieving *well* (whatever that means). 'When are you coming back to the stage at Saddleback? 'We need you,' someone cluelessly said to me recently. Mourners are encouraged to quickly move on, turn the corner, get back to work, think of the positive, be grateful for what is left, have another baby, and other unkind, unfeeling, obtuse, and downright cruel comments.

"What does this say about us - other than we're terribly uncomfortable with death, with grief, with mourning, with loss – or we're so self-absorbed that we easily forget the profound suffering the loss of a child creates in the shattered parents and remaining children."

Within seven days, her post had gone viral with 3.75 million readers and 10,000 comments. Thousands of individuals shared stories of lost family members due to illness, suicide, or a tragic accident. They recounted the insensitivity of family and friends, and their own shame and guilt about their overwhelming grief. Kay's post is a good summary of what not to say to those in grief and why.

Most Americans just don't know how to grieve. Knowing the right thing to say doesn't come naturally to us. We weren't born with that skill, and nobody ever taught us, so we never learned. And since we don't know how to grieve, we don't know how to respond to others in their grief. We don't know what to say and not say. In addition, most of us haven't had much experience with people in deep emotional pain and it's not always apparent when we're helping or hurting them.

This concept can be scary, awkward, and downright perplexing. What feels right and helpful for one person may be all wrong for another. Likewise, the timing of when you say something may make all the difference. Or you might be the right person to say something to a friend or family member, but the wrong person to say it to another. I will be the first to admit I haven't always said the right things to those in grief but I'm learning. I invite you to learn with me. Below are three tips for talking to someone in grief followed by my top ten list of the best and worst things to say to those in grief.

Tip #1: It's Not About You

One of the greatest opening lines from a book came from Rick Warren, author of *The Purpose-Driven Life*, when he said, "It's not about you." Rick was referring to finding your purpose in life, but I want to apply it to what to say or not say to grieving people. Many people want to talk about how the grieving person's loss affects them. When someone shares their loss, it's important to listen and not to give your loss history. You may want to say, "Oh my gosh, my mother died last year, too. Let me tell you what happened." When your loved one dies, that's the only person you want to hear about.

Now, it's completely okay to say, "Oh my gosh, I've dealt with loss myself and I really want to be here for you." That puts the attention back on them. In responding to the loss of my daughter, I heard many people say, "Oh gosh, Dave, I could never handle what you are going through." These people meant well but it was more about them than me.

Tip #2: Avoid Bright Siding and Toxic Positivity

When people are in pain, we naturally want to help soothe the pain and lighten the mood. In principle, it's a kind gesture, but in reality, it's never welcome. Be careful of bright siding and serving up toxic positivity. Bright siding is forced gratitude. It sounds like this: "Aren't you glad they died so quickly?" "Be happy that she is at peace now." "Everything happens for a reason." Be fully present with someone in grief without trying to point out the silver lining.

"When life gives you lemons, make lemonade" is a phrase meant to encourage optimism in the face of adversity. Lemons suggest sourness or difficulty in life; when applied to grief, lemons could suggest sadness. Hence, the goal for many is to turn sadness into something positive. But the way lemons are turned into lemonade is by sugarcoating them, making them seem more positive than they really are. Avoid sugarcoating someone's grief. Let them feel the sadness and pain that accompanies grief without trying to brighten things up.

Toxic positivity is positivity given in the wrong way, in the wrong dose, and at the wrong time. It sounds like this: "Cheer up!" "Buck up!" "Dig deep!" "Don't worry!" "Stop focusing on the negative!" "Try to have a better attitude!" "Remember, God never gives us more than we can bear." We often go overboard on positivity because we don't want people that we care about to feel bad. We sometimes say stupid things because we are uncomfortable in our own pain.

When you've lost a loved one, you're in a dark, raw place. Nothing anyone can say is going to cheer you up, especially conversations that begin with the words "at least." "At least she isn't suffering anymore." "At least he died doing something he loved." "At least she's in a better place." If you're going to start off a sentence with "at least," just stop yourself. It's not going to be helpful. You're trying to force them to look at the positive when they're feeling horrible. Learn to respond and not just react by saying the first thing that comes to your mind. Self-reflection and awareness are key.

Tip #3: Listen Without Judging

Grief is a no judgment zone. There is no right way to grieve. It's an individual process. When I'm with someone who's loved one has died, I try to validate what they are feeling. Not to judge it or try to change it—just to acknowledge it fully. Don't tell a grieving person how to feel. They may need to be vulnerable. They may need to cry for days on end. I feel honored when someone shares their pain and grief with me. The act of witnessing their vulnerability can bring the person out of isolation if the witnessing is done without judgment. It's not your job to stop their grief and pain and make them feel better. Just let them feel.

The Worst Things to Say to Someone in Grief

1. I know how you feel.

No, you really don't know how they feel after their loss, even if it's the same type of loss you've experienced. People think they can understand another's heartbreak, but the reality is I can't understand the loss you're going through. I can't understand your sorrow. However, I can come alongside you and be present with you in your pain.

2. At least she lived a long life.

Many people die young, so they reason that your loved one lived a long life, and therefore, you shouldn't feel that bad. Even if your mother passes away at 94 years old like mine did, it still hurts.

3. He is in a better place.

This may be true, and heaven is a wonderful place, but it's just not the right time to say it. The thought that someone's loved one is better off deceased and without them can feel cruel.

4. There is a reason for everything.

One of my favorite verses in the Bible is Romans 8:28, "And we know that in all things God works for the good of those who love him." I personally find great comfort in this verse and so do millions of others but it's just not the right time to say it.

5. Aren't you over him yet? He has been dead for a while now.

Grief is not something that we get over even if it's been years since our loved one died.

6. You can still have another child.

This is often said to parents who have lost a child. It was said to me and Carrie numerous times. Biologically, we still could have had another child together, but we already had two other incredible children when Jackie died, and this was the last thing on our minds. It implied to me that Jackie was replaceable. My first death experience occurred when I was five years old when my hamster died. I loved my little hamster and cried a river of tears when he died because it hurt deeply. My dad went to the pet store the same day and bought me another hamster. Children aren't hamsters.

7. She was such a good person that God wanted her to be with him.

Sometimes people say, "God needed another angel." God doesn't need any more angels. Your loved one does not become an angel when they die. If God needed more good people in heaven, then why are some of us still here?

8. He brought this upon himself.

Maybe a loved one died from suicide or an accidental drug overdose. We don't know the whole story and to say, "He brought this on upon himself" is cruel and never welcomed.

9. She did what she came here to do, so it was her time to go.

Well, maybe she did but maybe she didn't. We don't know for sure. What I do know is that saying that isn't going to soothe someone's pain or help them in their grief.

10. Be strong for your family and dig deep.

Often people say, "Lean on God." It's good to lean on God but just not the right time to say it. One translation of saying, "Be strong for your family" is "Don't have those sad feelings." For many men when they are told, "Your family needs you to be strong," instead, they hear, "Don't grieve." As men, we've been taught not to cry or show our emotions. We all need to grieve, especially men.

A Well-Meaning Friend

After my daughter's diagnosis, our church staff and elders came over to our house to pray for my daughter's healing. It was a sweet moment. One staff member approached me after the prayer and said, "Dave, you don't have to worry because God showed me that he's going to heal your daughter and all you need to do is have faith." I so wanted to believe what he said, yet in my heart, I felt she may die as I observed her progressing in her cancer and knew that unless God intervened, she would die.

Please be cautious of what I call *religious gobbledygook responses*. This refers to pompous, pretentious, and nonsensical jargon. Be careful with religion. I say that as a person of faith and as a pastor. Imposing your religious beliefs, feelings, or wishes on others can be hurtful. This is an extreme case of what not to say but it illustrates how we can get caught up in our own emotions. Kay's friends meant well and so did my friend, but we need to use extreme caution in what we say to those in grief.

We've examined the worst things to say, now, let's look at the best things to say to those in grief. The most important things you can remember is to keep your condolences simple and to speak from the heart. It's brave and it's hard to do but so necessary to make this world a kinder place. Don't try to say the perfect thing. Express sympathy from your heart, and you'll never go wrong with an authentic message of love and support.

The Best Things to Say to Someone in Grief

1. I am so sorry for your loss.

This phrase is simple yet powerful. If you don't know what to say, just say, "John, I'm so *sorry* for your loss." You don't have to elaborate, just express your sadness for their loss. I don't say, "My condolences for your loss." It sounds too formal and businesslike to me.

2. That must really hurt.

This phrase sounds strange and is different from how we normally approach helping someone in grief. We want to play it down and take their minds off the pain, but they desperately need to say what hurts and have their pain understood. This shows you are empathic.

3. I wish I had the right words; just know I care.

This phrase shows your humility and compassion. You're admitting you don't know what to say, that you don't have the right words, but that you deeply care for the person in grief.

4. I don't know how you feel, but I am here for you to help in any way I can.

This phrase shows your vulnerability and honesty. "I don't know how you feel but I want to walk this grief journey with you and help you in any way I can."

5. You and your loved one will be in my thoughts and prayers.

Prayer is powerful. Letting someone know you care for them and are praying for them in their pain is one of the best things you can do for someone who is grieving the death of a loved one.

6. My favorite memory of your loved one is…

After my daughter died, I loved to hear stories about her that I didn't know about. It might have been her teacher, or a friend, or one of Jackie's friends who would share memories about my daughter with me. Those stories are precious and show the thoughtfulness of the person sharing them. People are often hesitant to bring up my daughter's name or to share a story about her. I only wish they knew how much joy hearing about my daughter brings to my heart and soul.

7. I am always just a phone call away.

This is a positive phrase that shows you're wanting to practically help them in their time of need when they're ready for your help. It lets them know that you are available to them, day, or night. "Call me or text me anytime."

8. Give them a hug instead of saying something.

I call this the ministry of presence. No words. Just a warm embrace that shows you truly care means the world to people.

9. We all need help at times like this. God is with you, and I am here for you.

This lets your friend know that God loves them, is present with them, and that you will be with them, too. This shows that you are a loyal friend.

10. Saying nothing; just be with the person.

People don't need our words as much as they need our presence. When Pastor Bill lost his father, his associate pastor, Don, drove 180 miles to the graveside service and stood at the grave site, wrapped his arms around Bill, and wept with him for five minutes before walking away. He didn't say a single word. Bill will remember that embrace until he goes to his own grave.

Three Meaningful Responses to People in Pain (The 3 H's)

It's vital that we give people permission to grieve their loss and to provide a safe place for them to talk about what hurts the most. Grieving people are searching for safety because there is nothing safe about loss. The most important gift we can give people is our presence. In my work as a pastor, we call this the ministry of presence. Presence is the act of being with another person, with your full attention and engagement.

Doug Manning describes three impactful responses we can offer to those in grief. They can be remembered as the *3 H's*: 1) Hang around, 2) Hug, and 3) Hush.[2] Those in grief need our presence; nothing takes the place of being there. They also need our hugs. Nothing feels better than a hug when we are hurting. And most of all, they need us to hush. That is the hardest one of all.

Hang Around

Hanging around grieving people includes standing by them through active listening, compassion, and empathy. When you genuinely listen, people will realize you care about them. Listening to their stories and saying the name of the deceased lends support to one who is grieving.

Hug

Hugs are one of the most powerful tools we have as human beings to bring comfort to our loved ones. A simple hug can convey more than words ever can. After a significant loss, grieving people who are visited, hugged, and touched often report feeling comforted and supported. They experience a sense of connection that helps them continue to search for meaning and purpose in life.

Since touch is physical, it has bodily effects. Hugging helps lower blood pressure, reduces the risk of heart disease, heart attack, and stroke. Hugs also release feel-good chemicals in the body and boost our self-esteem. Touch is a powerful language to express feelings of safety, love, and connection to people. When we are touched in comforting ways, our brains are flooded with dopamine, serotonin, and oxytocin. These feel-good hormones help regulate our mood and make us feel calmer and happier. When we aren't touched, our brains suffer from the lack of these chemicals and we may feel depressed, anxious, stressed, and have trouble sleeping.

I'll never forget how comforting it was to receive hugs from my church family and friends immediately after Jackie's funeral service concluded. A few of the Saddleback staff flew up to Sacramento for the service and I still remember the warm feeling I got inside when Kay Warren, Tom, and Chandel Holladay hugged me. And of course, the hug master himself, Rick Warren, is a tremendous hugger. Pastor Rick understands the power and significance of personal touch and the impact of hugs.

Donna, a friend and singer from Sonrise Church, recently battled breast cancer and received intense chemotherapy treatment. She thought, *I need a hug from Pastor Dave.* So, she asked God in prayer for such a hug. That night, she had a dream: "I was at a work conference and in walks this tall man wearing a blue suit. It was Pastor Dave and I fell into his arms, crying uncontrollably!" She felt this was the answer to her prayer. Donna didn't pray for a sermon from me but a hug. People remember your hugs more than your sermons. Author Maya Angelou said, "People will forget what you said… but people will never forget how you made them feel."

A father from Saddleback Church died in a motorcycle accident during the pandemic, so we had to virtually plan his memorial service. He left behind his wife and two kids, a boy and a girl. His memorial service was held outside at our Rancho campus and limited to ten people in attendance. When the family arrived, the 18-year-old daughter made a beeline for me and came toward me with tears in her eyes and arms wide open, expecting a hug. How would I respond considering the health crisis? We were advised not to touch anybody. On top of that, I am immunocompromised. Even with the possibility of getting COVID-19 myself, I felt like she needed a hug. I hugged her and we wept together.

Hush

When you're trying to help someone in pain, please remember this: The deeper the pain, the fewer the words you use. The reality is you don't need to say anything. Just show up and shut up. You can't talk people out of their pain. Some pain is beyond words. When it's the right time, the hurting person will speak. Then, you'll be able to say something to them, as well.

Sitting Shiva was part of the mourning process in Judaism. The Hebrew word *shiva* means seven. Shiva lasted for seven days when a person died. After the initial mourning and burial, mourners would sit in their homes as visitors came to give comfort. We see this in the book of Job when his friends came and sat next to him on the ground for seven days after his loss and initially didn't say a word. It was when they opened their mouths that harm was done. We need to learn how to trust presence, touch, and silence.

In the next chapter of *The School of Grief*, you will learn about the relationship between faith and grief and how faith can be an anchor to your soul when you are in deep pain because of a loss.

CHAPTER 7:
FAITH AND GRIEF

> *"Grief is like going through a tunnel and sometimes we wonder if we'll ever come out the other end. But God has not abandoned you, and He wants to comfort you and assure you that he is with you."*
> *Billy Graham*

I don't always understand God. When I lost my daughter to brain cancer, not only did the loss challenge me to the core but it also confused me because I prayed for six weeks and believed in my heart that God was going to heal her.

I honestly thought I would see God miraculously heal my daughter, yet she ended up digressing and passed away in my arms. I believed, yet God didn't do what I asked Him to do. I've talked with many people who also struggle with the same issue of God not doing what they asked of Him. Some people might suggest that God didn't heal your loved one because you didn't have enough faith. That isn't the case. I think it takes more faith to trust God after a significant loss than it does if your loved one is healed.

After Jackie died, I felt sad, abandoned, angry, frustrated, and disappointed because I expected something different. I asked, "Why me? Why her? Why did this happen?" I expected a different life than the one I was living after my loss. Some people abandon their faith and walk away from God when tragedy strikes. They think if God really loved them, He wouldn't allow misfortune in their lives. I've had my ups and downs in my relationship with God, but I never doubted His love for me. Although I couldn't see a positive outcome, I trusted God for a good outcome in the end. Why? Because God is good, and His plans are good.

God never promises that what we experience in this life will be good. We live in a sin-stained world. We shouldn't expect heaven on earth because this earth is filled with brokenness. But even in the middle of all the brokenness, God has a good plan for your life.

Romans 8:28

Paul said, "And we know that in all things God works for the good of those who love Him, who have been called according to His purpose" (Romans 8:28). This verse is a promise. God is working with us to bring about good in our lives. I think if we were honest we'd say, "Sometimes this verse has been a great comfort to me and other times it's stretched my faith to the point where I want to tear it out of my Bible. Have you ever felt like that?" Yeah, right, God! You're going to take this loss in my life and eventually turn it into something good? Really?"

Author A.W. Tozer said, "What comes into our minds when we think about God is the most important thing about us."[1] When you go through a hard time, your theology about

God and what you think about Him matters. Do you think of God as sovereign, loving, and good? King David said, "Taste and see that the Lord is good" (Psalm 34:8). God is good and has the power to turn our hardships into something good. I can look back two decades now and say that God's plans for me were good, even considering the loss of my daughter.

Three Categories of People

All of us live in one of three primary locations in relationship to pain.[2] I've observed there are three categories of people in relation to Romans 8:28. Some of you are what I refer to as BPs. You are *Before Pain* people. Some can live the first 15, 20, or 30 years without tragedy coming their way. And if you're BP, Romans 8:28 to you is a *Theory*.

Some of you, are currently right in the middle of pain. You're IPs. You're *In Pain* people. Whenever you read this verse it's a *Lifeline*. You think, "If this verse wasn't in my Bible, I would think the world's out of control. But with this verse I'm hanging on because I know something good is going to come out of my pain. So, I'm leaning into God and trusting him to do something redemptive in my life."

And the rest of us are APs, *After Pain* people. We're in the process of healing and recovering from our pain. For those of us who have been through deep pain and are on the backside now, Romans 8:28 is a *Treasure*. God's promise in this verse is an absolute gift to me and to many of you.

When my wife bakes a cake, I've noticed the individual ingredients, flour, raw eggs, and vanilla don't taste good by themselves. But when she mixes them all together and exposes them to heat it tastes great. When you let God work all the ingredients together, He can turn your life into a masterpiece.

God is Close to the Brokenhearted

When Jackie died, I felt confused, abandoned by God, angry at the Almighty, and utterly disoriented. I was confused about my relationship with Him, my identity, and my future. I felt so alone. Why did God seem so distant when I needed Him most?

I found relief and comfort when I turned to the book of Psalms, specifically Psalm 34:18: "The Lord is close to the brokenhearted and saves those who are crushed in spirit." David says God understands our feelings and helps us bear our burden of sorrow. In contrast to other gods, or the unfeeling universe of atheism, the God of the Bible deeply cares for our pain.

David begins by saying, "The LORD," which is in all caps referring to Yahweh, the Creator of Everything and the great I AM. He says the LORD is close to the brokenhearted. Where is God when it really hurts? Maybe He's closer than we think. God is very close to you after your loss. In fact, David is implying that God is standing right beside you. He meets you in your deepest pain.

I like Eugene Peterson's paraphrase of this verse: "If your heart is broken, you'll find God right there; if you're kicked in the gut, he'll help you catch your breath" (Psalm 34:18 MSG). Peterson says, "You'll find God *right there*." The NASB version says, "The Lord is *near* to the brokenhearted. And saves those who are crushed in spirit."

David says God is not only present with us, but nearby. Near to the pain we feel, to the loss we can't fill, and to the feelings we can't express in words. For the brokenhearted, God gives nearness.

God is not distant or removed from knowing about our pain and unique experience of loss. He is always available and close to those who suffer. Not only is He near, but He stays with us and helps us get through our pain.

He Saves Those Who Are Crushed in Spirit

David says God saves (rescues or delivers) those who are crushed in spirit. The Psalmist isn't referring to the New Testament concept of salvation, which includes forgiveness from sin and a right standing with God. Rather, he's referring to the Old Testament concept of salvation that includes delivering us or rescuing us from our troubles and pain. It's freedom from distress and the ability to live again.

God will give you the courage, strength, and ability to live again. As I reflect on that season in my life, I now realize that I never felt closer to God than during my daughter's illness and death and the days that followed. My faith in God sustained me in grief. I didn't know what my future held but I knew I wouldn't face it alone.

Isaiah said, "When you go through deep waters, I will be with you. When you go through rivers of difficulty, you will not drown. When you walk through the fire of oppression, you will not be burned up; the flames will not consume you" (Isaiah 43:2 NLT).

There is nothing to fear when God is near. On your own, you might drown in your grief, but God said He will never leave you nor forsake you (Hebrews 13:5). I didn't doubt God's love for me, but I did doubt His sovereignty. Was He really in control by allowing my daughter to die? But I figured if I walked away from God, where would I go?

Jesus asked Peter if he was going to leave him, to which Peter replied, "Lord, where would I go? For you alone have the words of eternal life" (John 6:68). God is the source of life and truth: "God is our refuge and strength, an ever-present help in trouble" (Psalm 46:1). I decided to lean into the God who is close to the brokenhearted and delivers those who are crushed in spirit. It's important to grieve freely and trust God to lead you through the darkness and heal your pain. My faith in God became an anchor to my soul during my sorrow.

Family Support

I've been blessed to have a loving and supportive family that starts with my wife, our kids, my parents, and my parents-in-law. This also includes my extended family, who have been there for me when I needed them.

Jackie's death was a profound turning point not only for my immediate family but also for our extended family. Losing Jackie changed our family dynamic forever. Overnight, Jessica went from being the middle child in the birth order to now being the youngest.

I'm so fortunate I didn't have to go through the grieving process alone. My wife was my grief companion. Although we couldn't offer a lot of comfort to each other because we were both running on emotional fumes, we knew we were in this together. We felt our relationship with God and our strong families would help us persevere through our loss.

My father, Dr. David E. Page, MD, died of a heart attack a year before Jackie's passing. He loved Jackie dearly and would have been distraught about her death. I'm thankful he never knew that pain but I'm sad he wasn't alive because he was my

FAITH AND GRIEF

biggest cheerleader and would have offered me and our family tremendous support.

My mother, Joanne Page, has had the greatest influence on my life. She was an anchor for my soul. She cried with me and was a calming influence during the storm. I really thought my mom would be able to fix the problem, to somehow figure out a way to get rid of Jackie's brain tumor. She always fixed problems when I was a kid, so why not this one? But I realized that was an unfair and unrealistic expectation. I witnessed her pain—a grandmother watching her granddaughter physically decline and die.

Joshua, my nine-year-old son, was so tender and loving toward me. He assured me that everything was going to be alright. Jessica, my seven-year-old daughter, comforted me with her kindness and hugs. My father-in-law, Frank, became like a second dad to me after I lost my own. He adored Jackie and losing her was exceptionally painful for Grandpa Finch. My mother-in-law, Janice, was a great help to our family during Jackie's illness and after her death.

After Jackie's diagnosis, our family gathered at our home to throw Jackie a surprise birthday party in February, even though her birthday is December 20th. The family knew Jackie would never have a birthday party again.

We all huddled in our home on a cold winter night as Carrie brought Jackie into our dark home. The lights came on and 30 family members yelled, "Surprise." Jackie looked delighted and a bit scared at the same time. She reached out her arms for me to pick her up and buried her head into my chest. "It's okay, Jackie. This is your surprise birthday party," I said. She smiled and then saw all the gifts the family members had brought her and a beautiful wedding cake with her name on it. What a memory. What a family.

Sharon, Carrie's oldest sister, was a health care administrator in Southern California and flew up to be with us during Jackie's last days. She was knowledgeable about the end-of-life process and the medications Jackie was receiving. Sharon let us know when Jackie was close to death.

Friends from Church

Most of my closest friends are from church. The Apostle Paul said, "Rejoice with those who rejoice; mourn with those who mourn" (Romans 12:15). Friends are called to come alongside others and share their burden. Paul also said, "Bear one another's burdens, and so fulfill the law of Christ" (Galatians 6:2). A burden in this verse is a heavy weight.

The idea of bearing one another's burdens is a picture of a man staggering beneath a heavy load of grain. Somehow, he must get the grain home to his family, but he is about to crumble underneath its weight. A friend sees his distress and rushes to his aid, lifting a part of the burden and thereby easing the weight. Although the supportive friend does not assume the whole load, his help allows the struggling brother to carry it to his destination. Friends help carry their friends' burdens.

Friends are essential in our grief because death makes us feel alone and exposed. We feel vulnerable when we lose a significant loved one. You find out who your true friends are after loss. Good friends will stick with you through thick and thin and will be there to support you in your grief. They are there for you when you need a shoulder to cry on, or a good distraction. It's important to spend time with your friends as a way of cheering yourself up. Friends don't let friends grieve alone.

Church Support

There is no perfect church. Pastor and author Charles Spurgeon said, "The day we find the perfect church, it becomes imperfect the moment we join it." Every church is flawed and made up of imperfect people, but the beauty of the local church is truly amazing. The church is the greatest hope in the world, now more than ever. When my daughter died, Sonrise Church was *the church* in all the right ways, in the best sense of the word. Our church family mourned with us, took us under their wings, and helped carry us in our grief and pain.

When I flew home after getting the news of Jackie's diagnosis, two friends from my men's small group, Mike and David, picked me up from the airport and drove me home. I'll always remember their presence with me when I was in shock from the news of my daughter's terminal diagnosis.

Weeks before Jackie's death, the church held an all-day prayer vigil for Jackie. People joined us in praying for her healing. After Jackie's passing, the church took a love offering for our family and raised $10,000 to help us pay for the funeral expenses.

Norm, a friend and leader in our church, brought his brand-new Dodge Durango over to our house the night before Jackie's funeral and suggested we use it to transport our family the next day. Norm and his wife, Phyliss, lost their 21-year-old daughter, Laurie, in a car accident over a decade before we met them. They became grief mentors to me and Carrie. Norm started a GriefShare group at his home a couple of weeks after Jackie died that we joined.

Christy, our Children's Director at church, came over during Jackie's illness and played catch with a baseball with Jessica. Christy knew that the focus was on Jackie and that Jessica needed love, as well. I'll never forget that act of compassion. Pastor Tim, my top associate pastor, was there for me during my pain and would ask, "How can I serve you?" Unbelievable.

The Nazarene Church in Auburn allowed us to use their worship center for the funeral because our worship center wasn't large enough to accommodate the crowd in one service. Our staff and volunteers did an amazing job helping plan the funeral. It was personal, meaningful, and memorable. Friends from other churches attended the funeral, including members from our first church plant, Harvest Church, and friends from Saddleback Church, along with pastors from other local churches in Auburn.

An Unexpected Gift

I received a letter in the mail the week after Jackie's death with a whole bunch of one-hundred-dollar bills inside with a note that said, "Take your wife to Hawaii." Who sends cash in the mail? Carrie and I went to Hawaii to get away, relax, and refuel after the worst season of our life.

I went to church the next morning at New Hope Oahu. Carrie stayed at our hotel. The pastor, Wayne Cordeiro, came out on stage to start the service and said, "We're thrilled today to have two tremendous singers from the mainland with us, Bryan Duncan and Matthew Ward.

God See Us in Our Pain

Bryan Duncan, a contemporary Christian artist and friend, sang a song called, *Strollin' on the Water* at my daughter's funeral a week earlier. He came out and sang the exact same song at the church. I started to cry in my theater seat in the worship center. The lady next to me asked if I was okay. In my deep pain, I felt like God had reached down and gave me a hug from heaven, reassuring me that He saw me, was with me, and loved me.

After the service, I approached Bryan as he was greeting people. "What are you doing here?" he asked.

"A friend suggested we come to get away," I replied.

"Come with me. I want to introduce you to Pastor Wayne," he said.

Bryan shared with Wayne about my loss. "What are you doing tomorrow morning?" Wayne asked.

"I'm free, why?" I replied.

He told me he'd like to treat me to breakfast at Royal Hawaiian Resort. We met for breakfast, and he shared about his sister's death when he was just 14 years old. Wayne, a total stranger until that morning, encouraged me and radiated hope.

Hagar, a woman in the Old Testament who had been abused, was thrown out of her house and left in the desert by herself. An angel of the Lord came and spoke to her and promised to bless her in her despair. She recognized that it was God speaking directly to her. From then on, she calls him, "The God who sees me." She says, "For I have seen the God who sees me" (Genesis 16:13).

Sometimes, the blessing is what happens on the inside of us in our relationship and faith in God who sees what we cannot. When we realize that God sees us in our sorrow, then we become more willing to trust Him with our pain.

Over the next few weeks, various families provided meals for our family. We received hundreds of cards, letters, and emails. The outpouring of love was overwhelming. I wasn't used to receiving help from others. I was a pastor and a caregiver who gave to others as much as possible, but I had nothing left to give. I was brokenhearted and embraced the help from our church family. I am forever grateful to our church family in Auburn for the extraordinary love and support they showed our family during our time of need.

In the next chapter of *The School of Grief,* you will learn some common myths about grief and the School of Grief's approach to grieving, which I believe is a better way to grieve. You will be introduced to The Seven Needs of the Grieving.

PART THREE:
THE SEVEN NEEDS OF THE GRIEVING

CHAPTER 8:
THE SEVEN NEEDS OF THE GRIEVING

The next several chapters identify and explain the seven needs that grieving people have after their loss. This list is not a complete list of every possible need that grieving people have but an overview of the essential seven needs for those experiencing loss, pain, and grief.

It's important to grieve fully so we can live fully. People who don't grieve fully get stuck in the grieving process. They walk around with internal wounds, which distort the way they live their daily lives. Some grief-laden people wind up in the ditches of alcoholism, workaholism, drug addiction, sex addiction, broken relationships, and other compulsive behaviors—all because of an inability to grieve in a healthy manner. If you grieve in a healthy way, you can live a healthy life after your loss. If you grieve in an unhealthy way, all bets are off.

Myths We Are Taught About Grief

John James and Frank Cherry, authors of *The Grief Recovery Handbook*,[1] illustrate some common myths we are taught about grief by tracing a boy named Johnny. When young

THE SEVEN NEEDS OF THE GRIEVING

Johnny's dog dies, Johnny is stunned, and bursts out crying. "Uh, don't feel bad, Johnny, we'll get you a new dog Saturday," responded his dad. In that one sentence, Johnny's dad offers two myths about dealing with grief: Bury your feelings; replace your losses.

Later Johnny falls in love with a high school girl, the world never looked brighter, until she dumps him. Johnny's heart is broken but mom comes to the rescue and says, "Don't feel bad, John, there are other fish in the sea." Translation: Bury the pain, replace the loss.

Much later, John's grandfather dies, the one he fished with every summer and felt close to. He received a note in his math class telling him about the sad news of his grandfather's death. He read the note and couldn't fight off tears. He broke down sobbing at his desk. The teacher felt uncomfortable about it and sent him to the school office to grieve alone.

When John's father brought him home from school, John saw his mother weeping in the living room, and he wanted to embrace her and cry with her. But his dad said, "Don't disturb her, John, she needs to be alone. She'll be all right in a little while. Then the two of you can talk." Here, we see another piece of the common myths grieving puzzle: grieve alone.

Eventually, he buried his feelings and replaced the loss of his grandfather with a whole host of athletic involvements. He tried to function normally but found himself thinking about his grandpa, the fishing trips, the Christmas Eves, and the birthdays. His dad said, "John, give it time." Translation: Time heals in and of itself. This concept that time heals grief is possibly responsible for more heartache than any other single myth about grief. It seems to get passed down from generation to generation.

John gave it more time, but somehow, he felt trapped in a cell of sadness. What made matters worse is that he realized he had never thanked his grandpa for the fishing trips, snacks for lunches, and the late afternoon swims when the fish weren't biting. He had left so many things unsaid, even the big one: "I love you, Grandpa." John said to himself, "What can I do about it now? I guess I'll just have to live with guilt and regret for the rest of my life." That's another common myth about grief, if there's unfinished business, plan to live with guilt and regret, there's nothing you can do about it.

John figured that the best way to make sure this kind of pain didn't happen to him again was to keep an arm's distance from any close involvement. Translation: Wall up and never trust again.

A short time later, John's grandmother died. John recalls a family meeting and being told, "We have to be strong for your brother." Translation: Be strong for others. What does that mean? It means don't be vulnerable, don't cry, or show your emotions.

I've given you a peek at some common myths about grief. I'm sure many of you have tasted one or more of these myths. Below is a summary about what this approach teaches us to do with our grief:

Common Myths About Grief

1. Grieve alone.

2. Bury your feelings.

3. Live with your guilt and regret.

4. Run from your pain.

5. Get over your grief quickly.

6. Don't expect to regain your purpose for living after loss.

7. There is no afterlife so you will never see your loved ones again.

These common myths leave us broken and wounded. Our modern Western culture has adopted an *aren't-you-over-it-yet?* attitude toward death and grief which is crippling. There's got to be a better way to grieve. The School of Grief provides a better way to grieve by identifying and explaining the seven needs of the grieving.

The School of Grief's Approach to Grief: The 7 Needs of the Grieving

Let me share a taste of a better way to grieve the loss of your loved one. The way I can

serve it up to you is by contrasting the common myths about grieving with a better way to grieve, point for point. The seven needs of the grieving are as follows:

1. To have your grief witnessed.

2. To feel your feelings.

3. To release your burden of guilt.

4. To face your fears.

5. To not get over it, but to grow into it.

6. To turn your pain into purpose.

7. **To hold onto the hope of heaven and your reunion with loved ones.**

Grieve Well to Live Well

When one of these seven elements is missing, we can become stagnant in the grieving process and experience undue pain. In the next seven chapters, the heart of this book, we will examine these seven needs in depth, chapter by chapter, one by one. I'll explain each need, share why it's important, how I've applied it in my life, and how you can apply it, as well. It's a healthy, hope-filled way to grieve that leads to a better way to live.

In the next chapter of *The School of Grief,* you will learn about the first need all grievers have: the need to have their grief witnessed and validated. You will also learn how you can give the gift of witnessing the grief to others.

CHAPTER 9:
TO HAVE YOUR GRIEF WITNESSED

> *"For the dead and the living, we must bear witness."*
> *Elie Wiesel (Holocaust survivor)*

Having our grief witnessed is the first of seven needs grievers have. Witnessing grief is the cornerstone, which the other six elements are built upon. This need is so fundamental that if you don't get your grief witnessed, it becomes impossible to progress on your grief journey. Grief requires witnessing.

Witnessing Grief

One Sunday morning at Saddleback Church, Jeff, a father, came to a worship service distraught. In desperation, he shared that Terra, his daughter, had just suffered the loss of her child. She had consistently gone to her obstetrician; everything looked fine until four days before her due date when the baby's heart stopped for some unknown reason. Terra had a stillbirth delivery. Weston Blake Pickett was born on March 27th. The excitement of a long-awaited pregnancy came to a shocking, unexpected, and painful end. This precious seven-pound, 20.5-inch baby boy was born without life as we know it. Terra and Brian, her husband, were devastated. In moments like this, we are cut to the deepest part of our soul.

Many mothers and fathers suffer the silent grief of miscarriage or stillbirth. Both terms describe pregnancy loss, but they differ according to when the loss occurs. In the United States, a miscarriage is defined as the loss of a baby before the 20th week of pregnancy, and a stillbirth is the loss of a baby at or after 20 weeks of pregnancy. The silence after a miscarriage or stillbirth is deafening and extremely painful. It's considered a private loss and a taboo subject worldwide linked to stigma and shame. Mothers and fathers grieve not only for their baby but also for all the dreams they had for their child.

I met with the couple, witnessed their grief, and let them share their pain. I asked them if they wanted to do a memorial for Weston. They were in shock and weren't sure whether they wanted to have a service. I shared that I would totally understand if they chose not to have one, but I also shared my bias that every person deserves to have their life celebrated including Weston. I knew how meaningful it would be for their family to have their grief witnessed.

I shared the words of King David with them from Psalm 139: "For you created my inmost being; you knit me together in my mother's womb... Your eyes saw my unformed body; all the days ordained for me were written in your book before one of them came to be" (Psalm 139:13,16).

I believe an unborn child is the blueprint for a fully formed human being—in this case, four days short of his due date.

The couple showed me a photo of Weston. He was breathtakingly beautiful with his dark brown hair and gorgeous facial features. He was wrapped in a blanket and looked like he was sleeping. They said they would pray about having a memorial or not.

A week later, they called me and confirmed that they wanted to have a memorial. We had it at the church. I performed the service, and many of their family and friends came to witness their grief and to honor the life of Weston Pickett. Jeff and Brian spoke along with other family members and friends. We sang, cried, laughed, prayed, and did a slideshow of the family, including photos of Weston and his new nursery that the couple built for him in their home. I could feel the healing beginning to take root as a result of having their grief witnessed at the memorial service. Terra and Brian will never regret having a memorial service for their precious son.

Hardwired to Have Our Grief Witnessed

Human beings are social and emotional beings designed by God to live in community with others. As emotional creatures, we have an innate need to have our grief witnessed by others. This need is hardwired within us, since our emotions bond us to one another, and those connections are the key to our survival.

We want everybody to see our grief and respond to what has happened to us. When a child is injured—say, they skin their knee—they look to their parents for help. That help often comes in the form of a boo-boo kiss, a light kiss on the injury to make the pain go away. Kids want their injury to be seen, their pain to be heard and validated by their mom, dad, and everybody around them, and so do we.

My friend, David Chrzan, a pastor, and adventurer, broke his femur in his right leg while riding his mountain bike in a canyon in Orange County. I visited him in his hospital room after his surgery to repair his leg.

After discussing the circumstances of his accident and prayer, I was getting ready to leave when he asked me, "Would you like to see my scar from the surgery?"

"No, that's okay, I replied. He was insistent on showing me his scar as he turned on his side and lifted his hospital gown, revealing a foot-long incision with stitches on the outside of his leg just below his hip.

"The surgeon inserted a couple titanium rods into my leg that will graft with the broken bone as it heals," David explained.

"That's cool," I replied. Maybe it's a guy thing, but we like to show our scars as a badge of honor after our accidents. I was the same way with my family and friends after my motorcycle and bicycle accidents. We want to have our pain witnessed and validated by others. It's the same way with grief; we need our pain witnessed.

David Kessler writes, "Each person's grief is as unique as their fingerprint. But what everyone has in common is that no matter how they grieve, they share a need for their grief to be witnessed. That doesn't mean needing someone to try to lessen it or reframe it for them. The need is for someone to be fully present to the magnitude of their loss without trying to point out the silver lining."[1]

In the School of Grief, we begin to witness grief by acknowledging a person's loss and letting them know they are seen. It's saying, "I see you and hear your pain. Your grief is real. It's genuine." Witnessing people's pain empowers them to feel supported and less alone. Observing grief allows grievers to focus on grieving their loss rather than grieving the loss of the support they need most.

It's important to create space for grievers to share their painful feelings. Witnessing someone's grief is one of the greatest gifts you can give to someone in grief. Ask about their loved one, then listen and let them talk. I feel honored when someone shares their pain and grief with me. When we see our sadness reflected in the eyes of another, we know our grief matters. We get a glimpse—maybe for the first time since our loss—that we will survive, and that a hope-filled future is possible.

Witnessing grief is about meeting people where they are and accepting them without trying to change them. We come with no agenda, judgment, or shame. Witnessing grief helps people develop a sense of comfort during the painful and negative feelings that accompany loss.

Can I Get a Witness?

This phrase is commonly used in African American churches and has a spiritual connotation: When the pastor asks, "Can I get a witness?" he's asking the congregation for affirmation which is often met with a response of "Amen!" I've had the privilege of preaching in a predominantly black church and it's inspiring to receive encouraging participation from the congregation. It fired me up and made me a better preacher when they would say, "Amen" or "Go on." The word *amen* means "it is true" or "so be it."

Witnessing affirms the griever and declares their loss is true and genuine. It's simple: When someone tells you their story about loss, your job is to witness their grief. Be present with them without thinking about yourself and what you might say next. Just listen and witness. Our world needs more witnessing. Can I get an amen?

Stop the World from Spinning

My world stopped at 9:40 a.m. on March 4 when my daughter died. It seemed strange that the clocks of the world continued when my inner clock stopped. After Jackie died, I wanted the world to come to a screeching halt to acknowledge the loss of my daughter. When it didn't happen, I wanted to scream, "Don't you understand that we're in deep pain here and our family's life has changed forever?" At least they could have flown flags at half-mast around the world to display our grief. In my mind, Jackie's death was just as important as any government official's death. It's hurts to watch the world keep spinning for everyone else when your heart has a hole the size of Texas in it and such a bright light has gone out.

A Unique Way of Witnessing Grief

I love how one tribe in particular witnesses grief when someone in their village dies. Kessler was touring Australia when he met a researcher that shared about her study of the Indigenous people's way of life in northern Australia. On the night someone dies, everyone in the village moves a piece of furniture or something else into their yard. The next day, when the bereaved family wakes up and looks outside, they see that everything has changed since their loved one died, not just for them but for everyone in the village.[2] This shows the grieving family that their loved one's death matters. It's a tangible witness as it makes the loss visible. Our world needs more furniture movers.

Witnessing Grief at a Funeral

Funerals are vital for having our grief witnessed. I never realized how meaningful a personalized funeral that accurately reflects your loved one's life could be until after my daughter's death. After meeting with families and performing hundreds of funerals, I'm convinced that a funeral ceremony done well can be the first step toward healing for a bereaved family. Funerals, memorials, and graveside services matter. Something magical happens when others gather to see, hear, feel, and witness our grief.

The funeral is the oldest and most familiar ritual in the world. Rituals unite us. Funerals are for the living, for those who remain. It's an important psychological step within the grieving process and helps bring closure. Funerals allow us to pay tribute to our loved one's life and help survivors face the reality of death. Funerals assist us in beginning the mourning process, expressing our beliefs, thoughts, and feelings, and saying goodbye to our loved one. Funerals give people an opportunity to support the family by demonstrating their love and respect for the deceased.

Significance

When loss happens, the first thing we need to do is establish the significance of that event. Significance is a key concept in witnessing grief. The hardest part of grieving is finding a way to establish significance. Friends and family are not comfortable with talking about death, pain, and loss. Yet, we want people to know about our loss and respond to it in an empathetic way without trivializing it.

Doug Manning, author of *The Funeral*, gives three levels of significance that need to be fulfilled after loss.[3] *First, we need to establish the significance of our loss.* This is what has happened to me. The first thing we think about when someone dies is ourselves. This sounds strange, doesn't it? We think, "What's going to happen to me now?" That's not selfish; it's survival. God designed us with a tremendous capacity to survive. We need to share what happened to us because of our loved one's death.

The second level is the need to establish the significance of the person we have lost. We want to tell everybody about the person we lost and show photos of them: "I need to tell you who this person was, what they meant to me, and how significant they were."

The third level is the social significance. This is one of the major reasons for having a funeral and why funerals are so important. The funeral is a time to gather so friends can tell us how much our loved one meant to them.

Funerals provide a network of support for grieving families. Funerals have become the new family reunions. Relatives you haven't seen in years travel great distances to attend the service.

On the other hand, when a family decides not to hold a funeral or service, it's a missed opportunity to have their grief witnessed, and for their friends to show their love and support. Failing to have a memorial service can lead to an increase in unresolved grief for years to come.

TO HAVE YOUR GRIEF WITNESSED

Auggie Pullman, from the movie *Wonder,* said, "I think there should be a rule that everyone in the world should get a standing ovation at least once in their lives." I wish everybody could get a standing ovation and feel the affirmation of their colleagues, family, and friends but very few people get this chance. I've done funerals where family and friends gave the deceased a standing ovation at the end of the service. Too bad we don't do it while the person is alive rather than waiting until they're dead to show our appreciation.

I think there should be a rule that everyone in the world should have a personalized funeral service. Why? Because I believe in the dignity of every human being. God created each person in His image and therefore, every person has value. All people matter to God. Every life is worth remembering and celebrating. To deny a person a funeral is to deny them an act of dignity.

Having Our Grief Witnessed at Jackie's Funeral

We had a viewing of Jackie's body the night before her funeral. The wake was only for family and close friends. Jackie appeared to be peacefully asleep in the casket. She looked cherub like in her beautiful white dress and ruby red slippers. Reality sinks in quickly when you see your little angel laying in a child-sized white casket on a dark spring night.

Our family had been at the wake for a couple of hours, and we were getting ready to go home when my sister, Suzy, and her husband, Mark, along with their month-old baby, Alex, walked into the room. There was a noticeable silence when my sister's family entered. Jackie was lying ever so still in the casket. You could hear a pin drop. Out of the silence came a loud cry from Alex, which pierced the stillness and broke the silence. It was music to my ears.

Amid our despair, there was hope. One child dies and another is born. One child's last breath was taken and another's first breath was given. The circle of life was staring us in the face. Jackie had died. Alex was alive and full of life.

The Value of a Funeral

A funeral is an important way to have your grief witnessed. Jackie's funeral was a fantastic celebration of her short life. She was so full of life and joy. I wanted everybody to know what a special little girl she was and that her life was not lived in vain but had significance.

Our family, friends, and staff at church worked together to create a custom-made funeral service that celebrated and honored her life. Workers made a beautiful rainbow balloon arch over the casket. Jackie's favorite movie was *The Wizard of Oz*, so it was breathtaking to view the rainbow over her casket and later hear the song, *Somewhere Over the Rainbow*. What many didn't realize was Jackie had always wanted ruby red slippers like Dorothy in the movie. So, we made sure she was buried in her ruby red slippers.

My fondest memory of the service was having our grief witnessed by nearly a thousand people including our closest friends, family, and church. I'll never forget that day for as long as I live. The love and support were overwhelming. Following the service, they had an impromptu reception line for our family as people came up and hugged us. Folks were unbelievably kind and compassionate toward us that day as they witnessed our grief. This demonstration of love and empathy helped carry us through the darkest time in our lives. I didn't know if I could do the eulogy, but God gave me strength. The memorial service was lovely and marked the beginning of our healing.

Should Children Attend Funerals?

I believe funerals are valuable for children as well as adults. My son, Joshua, attended his grandfather's funeral when he was eight years old. It was important for Joshua to be at the service. I think your child's wishes are a helpful guideline when making your decision. It was an open casket funeral, which is rare these days, and he wanted to go forward at the end to see his grandpa in the casket. Both of my kids attended Jackie's funeral service. Joshua was nine and

Jessica was seven. I couldn't imagine not letting them be there to say goodbye to their sister.

There is no right or wrong age to attend a funeral. Young kids can benefit from being involved in a funeral and having a chance to say farewell to their loved one. Let your child know what to expect at the funeral. Prepare them ahead of time as to what it will look like, how to dress, and what the schedule of the day will be. As I've talked with adults about this topic, many were denied attending funerals as children and wished they had been allowed to do so.

Witnessing Grief at a Wedding

My daughter, Jessica, got married recently. This was a big deal for the Page family. She is the first of our three children to do so. I asked her if she wanted me to walk her down the aisle as her father or if she wanted me to perform the wedding ceremony as a pastor and wedding officiant. "Dad, I want you to do both," she replied.

She asked seven girls to be her bridesmaids. I wondered who her maid of honor would be. She decided Jackie, her younger sister, would be her maid of honor. I got a bit teary-eyed when she told me. Matt, her fiancé, hand carved a small wooden bench that held a frame with Jackie's photo in it and a bouquet of flowers. Engraved on the bench were the words, "Jacqueline Brooke Page." The bench, photo, and flowers were positioned right next to the bride where the maid of honor normally stands.

Here is what I said after the welcome: "We are thrilled to have most of our family members here from both sides of the family, but we also want to remember a family member who can't be here today, someone who is not physically with us but is with us in spirit, most notably the maid of honor, none other than Jackie Page, Jessica's sister.

"When Jessica chose her bridesmaids, I kept asking her, 'Who's going to be your maid of honor?' She wouldn't tell me. Finally, a couple of weeks before the wedding, she said, 'Jackie is going to be my maid of honor.' We have a photo of Jackie on top of this bench, which is strategically placed in the maid of honor's spot. Jackie absolutely adored her sister, so it's natural that Jessica would have Jackie be her maid of honor. So, Jackie, we remember you today and our love for you never ends."

There wasn't a dry eye at the ceremony, with tears of sadness and tears of joy beautifully mixed together as our family had our grief witnessed some twenty years after Jackie's death. Witnessing grief lasts a lifetime because love never dies.

At the end of the celebration, Jessica came up to me and said, "Dad, this is the happiest day of my life." I was elated. I'm sure Jackie was smiling down on us from heaven that day.

Witnessing Grief During the Holidays

It's extremely important to have your grief witnessed during the holidays. The holidays are associated with family. The most wonderful time of the year can also be the most difficult time of the year for those who grieve. It's at this time we became acutely aware of the void in our lives. How do we have Christmas without Jackie? To make matters worse, Jackie's birthday was on December 20th. She was our Christmas baby.

Church services went on, Christmas carols were still sung, and people wished everybody a Merry Christmas. But my thoughts were on Jackie, fixed more on her departure than on her arrival five years prior. Christmas was different that first year without our daughter. We hung a stocking for her, talked about her, lit a candle in her memory, and shed many tears. Sometimes, showing up for something is the best you can do. We showed up that first Christmas and that was good enough.

Talk About Your Loved One

Maybe the best way to have your grief witnessed during the holidays is to talk about your loved one. We talk about the weather, food, sports, and work. We talk about everything else... except the elephant in the room. We all know it's there. It has hurt us all. But we don't talk about the elephant in the room. I encourage you to introduce the elephant in the room. Oh, please, say her name. Please say "Jackie" again. For if we talk about her death, perhaps we can talk about her life. Nothing brings relief like hearing a good story about your loved one.

Memorialize Your Loved One

Find a way to remember your loved one and memorialize them during the holidays. It might mean lighting a candle, writing a letter to your loved one and placing it under the tree, or creating an ornament with your loved one's picture on it and hanging it on the tree. I know someone who created a memory book of their loved one. Create a new tradition in memory of your loved one. You can donate to a favorite charity in their honor. I do this each year for the HEART Africa ministry. You can also go online and create a tribute page for your loved one. These are all ways to express your love for your family member or friend and to have your grief witnessed.

Include the Children

Children feel confused, powerless, angry, and anxious during the holidays because of a death in the family. Kids grieve differently than adults. Our children need their grief witnessed during the holidays, as well. Be honest with them. Explain that it's okay for them to cry and for adults to cry, and that although they are feeling sad right now, they won't always feel this way. Figure out which part of the holiday tradition is most important to them. Try to involve them in memorial rituals. For example, ask them to draw or write their favorite holiday memories of the departed loved one.

Witnessing Grief During Milestones

I recently graduated from Biola University with my Doctor of Ministry degree. It was the culmination of years of research, hard work, and perseverance.

On the morning of my graduation ceremony, I couldn't help but think of Jackie and my dad. I made a video that I posted on my social media platforms expressing how sad and disappointed I was because they couldn't be there to witness my accomplishment. Although they weren't there physically, I felt their presence with me.

My success was due to their influence on my life. Jackie became my motivation to keep going when I wanted to give up. I started the program after she died to grow personally and become a more effective pastor, better able to serve those I work with in ministry. My dad supported me in all my ministry endeavors. I felt Jackie and my dad both smiling down on me from heaven as they witnessed my milestone with great pride that day.

Witnessing Grief During Birthdays and Anniversaries

It's tricky going through birthdays and anniversaries after a loss. My wife and I give two cards to each other for every birthday, one from us and one from Jackie. We also give two cards to each other on Mother's Day and Father's Day, and our wedding anniversary. I write Jackie's card like she used to write, the typical handwriting of a five-year-old. Jackie's birthday is always a special day in our family. We've had birthday cakes before, and we've lit candles in her honor.

The anniversary of her death has always been extremely difficult. It was Thursday, seemingly a day like any other day. I couldn't sleep the night before and was plagued by thoughts of my baby and how much I missed her. Why was the 10-year anniversary of her death harder than five years or nine? I didn't know. It just seemed so final.

THE SCHOOL OF GRIEF

I was on the road coaching a network of pastors in Minneapolis. I got up that morning and remembered that March 4th was the exact day ten years earlier that Jackie had passed away in my arms. It was a peaceful passing but the finality of her being gone was more than I could handle.

Carrie went to work that morning but after arriving, she broke down in tears. "What are you doing here?" her friends asked. They told her to go home.

I called her from Minneapolis. She was walking on a pier in Santa Barbara. "How are you doing?" I asked.

"Not good," she replied.

"Are you going to jump off the pier?" I asked.

"No, it's not that bad," she replied. But she was in terrible pain and so was I. I longed to hug her and hold her, but we were 1500 miles apart. We vowed the next year that we wouldn't be apart on Jackie's death day, so we could offer each other support in any way our emotional capacities would allow.

I shared with the twelve pastors I was coaching about the significance of this day. They graciously prayed for me and our family. It felt good to have my colleagues witness my grief. Joshua wrote a song that he digitally recorded in Jackie's honor. Jessica stayed home from school. Sometimes, you get ambushed by your emotions. There was something about the finality of living life for ten years without Jackie that blindsided us all.

Pet Loss

The loss of a pet can be extremely painful. Some pet owners find the grief associated with pet loss just as or even more challenging than the loss of a loved one. I can relate. I recently lost my 13-year-old pure breed Siberian Husky named Ari. I love my wife dearly, but Ari was the love of my life. People who haven't experienced the unconditional love and companionship of a pet may find it difficult to understand and validate the grief of the person who has. Those who lose a pet need to have their grief witnessed and validated, as well.

Bereavement leave from work isn't normally granted when a pet passes. Funerals for pets are becoming more common but are still not the norm. For these reasons, pet parents can feel isolated and misunderstood during their grief. When Ari died, it seemed like only those who love animals understand the magnitude of my loss. You can tell a lot about a person by how they treat animals. Solomon wrote, "Good people are good to their animals... bad people kick and abuse them" (Proverbs 12:10 MSG).

Making the decision to euthanize a pet can be gut-wrenching. Guilt is typically linked to losing a pet especially when the pet is put down. I cried for a long time after Ari died. I have a photo of her on my screensaver on my iPhone and think of her nearly every day. If you've lost a pet, your grief is valid. Please be kind to yourself and take the time to grieve. The lessons I share in this book about grief apply directly to you.

Launching a Grief Community at Saddleback

I was asked to do a memorial service for Mary Shriver at Saddleback Church. I met Mary a couple of weeks before she died while she was on hospice. On my first visit to the house, the siblings took me aside and asked if I'd do her memorial. I agreed. She died two weeks later. Her husband, Dennis, is a prince of a guy and loved Mary well for 50 years. He was lost after she died. He didn't know what to do and felt he'd lost his purpose for living. I performed Mary's Celebration of Life service, which was beautiful and helped the family have their grief witnessed.

I asked Dennis if he wanted to have coffee the next week at a local Starbucks. He agreed. We met every other week to talk about Mary and his grief. I couldn't do this for every grief person I counsel with, but I could do it for Dennis.

People like Dennis need to be part of a supportive community that can witness their grief because healing happens in community. We had a community for people suffering from addiction called *Celebrate Recovery*. We also had a community for people with mental health issues called *Hope for Mental Health*. Grief isn't a mental health issue unless it becomes acute. I thought, *Why not start a community for grieving people?* So, I launched a Grief Community called *Hope for Grief*. Nobody can get through grief alone. We were meant for community. We were never meant to be islands of grief.

We gather on a regular basis to provide hope, encouragement, training, and connection with a caring community. I teach at these events, and we bring in guest speakers, who are grief specialists. We have a segment called *Music and Grief*, a form of grief therapy because music soothes our soul, *God and Grief,* which deals with theology, and one called *Hugged by God,* dealing with affirmations from God in our grief. We share a few of the best and worst things to say, along with testimonials, and a Q&A panel consisting of pastoral care pastors and licensed therapists.

A Witnessing Grief Exercise

At our first gathering, our topic was *The Power of Having Your Grief Witnessed.* I used an exercise I learned from Paul Denniston, founder of *Grief Yoga.*[4] I had people pair off at their tables and stand face to face with their partner. The first person who shared put his hand over his heart, looked the other person square in their eye, said the person's first name out loud, and then said, "I witness your pain and grief and I see your healing." This was a powerful exercise as many people were moved to tears and later shared with me it was the first time they had ever felt their grief witnessed.

Tips for Witnessing Grief in Others Below are three tips to help witness grief in others and provide a compassionate presence.

Depend Upon God for Help

When feeling overwhelmed, remember that God is with you in your pain. Don't run away from the discomfort but take a deep breath and lean into the sadness knowing God designed your body to grieve. Tears are welcome. Words are not necessary at first. Trust God to give you the appropriate words to say when the time is right: "The Holy Spirit will give you the words to say at the moment when you need them" (Luke 12:12).

Acknowledge the Pain

When witnessing a griever in pain, realize you don't have to fix them. Rather, seek to create a compassionate space for them without taking on their pain. Let them know that God sees them in their pain and so do you. Recognize that your presence alone, along with touch, is more powerful than words. Acknowledge their pain and validate that what they're going through really hurts. Let them know they don't have to hide or rush through their grief.

Show Empathy

Let grievers share their pain from their heart without judging or embarrassing them. Encourage them to express their feelings and embrace their pain. There's no need to look for a silver lining, but instead, perhaps share a good memory or story with them about their loved one. Let them share their feelings openly and remind them you are merely there to listen. People don't need our sympathy; they need empathy. Witnessing grief is to show empathy for how those in grief feel.

It takes enormous courage for a person to have their grief witnessed and to truly be seen when they feel wounded inside, when their heart is vulnerable and hurting. It also takes courage to witness the grief of another and view their tears and pain. As you witness grief, you become an openhearted healer. You give your family member or friend an incredible gift. Even though the act can be an emotionally exhausting experience; it's worth it. They will forever be changed.

May we first seek to understand, then to be understood. This approach supports the other person in their pain. It's what we all want and need, to be understood, valued, and affirmed in our grief. We all need to have our grief witnessed by someone who cares. I witness your grief and you witness mine. May we seek to witness the grief of others and have our grief witnessed within a caring community because healing comes in community, not in isolation.

In the next chapter of *The School of Grief*, you will learn about the importance of feeling your feelings, expressing your emotions, and embracing your pain in your grief.

CHAPTER 10:
TO FEEL YOUR FEELINGS

> *"You can't heal what you don't feel."*
> John Bradshaw

The second need we have as grievers is to feel our feelings. God is our creator and giver of emotions. He created us to grieve and designed us to feel our feelings and express our emotions.

Two guys from the mortuary came to our house after Jackie died. They parked the van at the bottom of our driveway and walked up to our house. It was time to take Jackie to the van. "We'll go get the gurney to carry her down to the van," one of them said.

"Guys, she's forty-two inches tall and only weighs about forty pounds. How about I just carry her down to the van instead?" I replied.

They agreed it was a good idea. I picked up her little body, carried it to the van, and laid her inside. The van drove down the road on St. Andrews Court, turned left onto Birch Way, and disappeared into the distance with our baby inside.

We stood there watching for what seemed like hours but was just a few minutes. We were in shock. Tears welled up in our eyes. We felt so helpless. So hopeless. Nothing in life prepared us for a moment like this. We had experienced a catastrophic loss and knew we were in deep weeds and needed help.

I didn't know what to do, where to turn, or how to deal with my pain. I called a Christian counselor in town to begin grief therapy. She shared with me the importance of expressing my emotions. She explained that God made our bodies to feel pain and that grief was a natural part of life. She encouraged me to process the pain I was feeling inside by crying into a pillow. She gave me grief homework to do.

I remember curling up in a fetal position and crying. I cried so hard and for so long to the point where I didn't think I could cry anymore. I was cried out. For a while, my tears just wouldn't come out. My tear ducks dried up. I had never experienced such a thing. I asked the counselor about it, and she said not to worry. She assured me that the tears would flow again when they were ready. And sure enough, they did.

I remember screaming into my pillow to release the pent-up anger inside. It was ugly. I screamed at the top of my lungs. I made guttural sounds I'd never heard myself utter before. It was like my soul was verbally vomiting and letting go of all the toxic stuff inside.

I remember howling like a wolf at the universe. I was crying so hard that I collapsed on the floor. I got up and looked in the mirror only to see my swollen eyes, tears on bright red cheeks, and drool running down my mouth. I was dehydrated, unable to stand, think, or walk. Sentences were hard to put together and didn't make sense.

Reoccurring Nightmares

I went back to the therapist for another appointment. I informed her that this grieving stuff was hard work. She smiled and said, "Yes, it is." I told her I didn't think I was doing very well. She

asked what my biggest challenge was. I shared that I was having nightmares every night of the two men from the mortuary driving my daughter away in the van. Each time I dreamed about it, I would wake up in a cold sweat.

"What can I do to get rid of the nightmares?" I desperately asked.

"Try reframing the situation. Instead of picturing two men taking your daughter away, imagine two angels coming down from heaven and gently taking Jackie home," she said.

Now, that sounded good. I gave it a try. The nightmares continued. I knew I needed further help.

Jerry Sittser's Wise Counsel

As I mentioned before, Jerry came and spoke at the weekend services at our church in Auburn. After lunch, I drove him back to the Sacramento airport. On the way, he asked me how I was doing in my grief? "Pretty well except that I keep having this recurring nightmare of watching the two men from the mortuary take my daughter away and disappearing," I replied.

TO FEEL YOUR FEELINGS

I shared about the advice given by the Christian therapist of picturing angels coming to take her away.

"How is that working for you?" he asked.

"It's not. I still have nightmares about it every night," I said.

"That crap didn't work for me either," Jerry said empathetically.

We burst into laughter together. I was surprised by his reply, but thankful for his honesty.

"Dave, you need to embrace the pain. You must feel the feelings to get better," he continued.

"How do you do that?" I asked.

"When the drunk driver hit our minivan, it was carnage, just awful. My four-year-old daughter died immediately from a broken neck. My wife was seriously injured but was still alive as was my mother. They both died a few minutes later. My six-year-old son had a broken femur and almost died, but thankfully survived. My other two kids were dazed, crying, and screaming but were relatively unhurt. It took an hour before the emergency vehicle reached us," he explained.

I was speechless as he shared the tragic details.

"You need to go back and relive the event in your mind, facing your fear and watching those two men drive away with your daughter. As crazy as it sounds, you embrace the pain. You feel the feelings all over again and let them sink in," he said.

My first thought was, *This sounds counterintuitive, but he certainly knows what's he's talking about, so why not give it a try?* I chose to relive the experience again and to feel the painful emptions associated with the experience. In my mind, I pictured the two men driving my daughter away from our home. I felt a piercing pain deep inside. I sat with my pain and let it marinate. I stayed in the moment, felt the feelings, and welcomed the pain streaming through my body.

I named my painful emotions and owned them. I felt my feelings to the core of my being despite the unpleasantness. I confronted the experience head on and felt a sense of dread over the finality that my daughter was gone for good.

After facing and embracing my pain, feeling my feelings, and expressing my emotions, the nightmares disappeared.

Feelings Matter

Author John Bradshaw in his book *Homecoming* said, "You can't heal what you don't feel." He saw a relationship between feeling and healing. If we don't name it, we can't feel it. And if we don't feel it, we can't heal it.

Acknowledging and naming feelings are the first steps to dealing with them and healing them. The process of becoming friendly with your feelings fosters growth and healing from your loss. Feelings can be harsh, so it's important to be kind to yourself in the grieving process.

Don't Bury Your Feelings

A hundred years ago, industrialists thought they could bury toxic waste and it would just go away. We've since learned that doesn't work. Rather, the waste leaks into the water, contaminates the crops, and kills animals. Burying grief does the same thing. It leaks into our emotional system and wreaks havoc. It distorts our perceptions of life, ruins our relationships, and keeps us stuck in our grief. My point is it's important to feel our feelings and not to bury them.

Our culture doesn't do a good job of teaching us how to deal with difficult emotions. It's intriguing to identify what you were taught about feelings as a child. As a boy, I was taught, "Big boys don't cry." As a high school basketball player, my coach told me "not to show emotion and not to talk back to referees," even if they made a bad call. Essentially, I was taught to stuff my emotions inside, erasing any trace of them completely.

The idea that emotions are something to stuff was woven deep inside my subconscious. I decided this understanding of emotions didn't serve me well as an adult. The death of my daughter forced me to examine my beliefs about emotions and to rewrite my own narrative about my feelings.

There's No Crying in Baseball

I love the movie *A League of Their Own*. A classic line is when Tom Hanks proclaims, "There's no crying in baseball!" In real life, some people, men in particular, are told not to cry. I'm here to tell you that's terrible advice. Don't let some macho saying prevent you from crying and from experiencing your subsequent healing. Crying, whether you are a man or woman, is actually very beneficial. I've learned to cry since the passing of my daughter. The good news is it really helps.

People are afraid to feel their feelings because they think they will be opening up Pandora's box of pain and that it will never end. This parable from Greek mythology that you don't want to open a box that could bring worse pain and suffering on you is just that, a myth. I remind grievers that we are *in* Pandora's box. We are experiencing pain and suffering in the moment.

We often forget the point of the parable. What remained after Pandora's box was opened was hope. Hope was in the box along with trouble and pain. Hope is found when we feel our feelings and express our emotions—the hope that no feeling is final, you won't cry forever, and when your feelings are felt they are then released.

Feel All the Feels

The key is to feel your feelings. I guarantee it's going to hurt, but every moment you're weeping, you're doing the work. Every moment you're hurting, you're healing. The only way out of the pain is through.

Do the Laps

Laird Hamilton is a big wave surfer—arguably the best of all-time. Big wave surfing is a discipline within surfing reserved for experienced surfers who paddle into, or are towed into, waves that are at least 20 feet high. Hamilton once shared that big wave surfers need to be in incredible shape to ride such big waves because when you wipe out, you can be under the water for minutes. To succeed, he says, "You have to do the laps."[1] He's referring to a training regimen of swimming many laps in a pool to build up the stamina and strength needed to save your life when you go down riding the big waves.

It's the same way with grief, which produces its own big waves. Swimming the laps in the pool is equivalent to identifying your feelings and feeling them. It's hard work but necessary to survive.

Pay Me Now or Pay Me Later

Feelings are an emotional state or reaction; they are vibrations of energy. There is power in feeling our feelings. Feelings say, "Pay me now, or pay me later, but you will pay." Grief will chase you down. Grief in the end will always get its way.

When you're grieving, you experience a wide variety of thoughts, feelings, and emotions. Your emotions may seem strange, but they are a true expression of where you are at the moment. Rather than denying your feelings or being victimized by them, learn to recognize, and learn from them. Trying to keep going in life suddenly didn't work anymore. I needed a different strategy. I decided to venture out of my comfort zone and to feel my feelings and express my emotions.

Ask yourself, "What am I feeling right now about my loss today?" Allow your thoughts and feelings to surface without judgment. Look your grief in the face and say hello to your feelings. I empower grievers to discover their feeling language and voice. Grievers often teach me about grief by explaining what they are feeling and experiencing in their soul. Grievers need space and encouragement to trust and express their feelings.

Express and Release Your Feelings

To express and release our feelings, we need to allow room for them to come out and be open to processing them. If we don't express our feelings and continue to suppress them, they will find their way out in other ways. Unfelt feelings don't just go away; they resurrect like a zombie in a horror movie.

Your emotions are data for your experience of life. If we ignore or repress our feelings, not only will they come out later, but we miss vital information about the origin of those feelings.

I had a great deal of anger after my daughter's death. I needed to feel it, express it, and get it out. I hit things and screamed a lot. We all need to find ways to express and release our feelings. When Forrest Gump lost Jenny, his wife and the love of his life, in the movie *Forrest Gump*, he began to run across the country to deal with his grief. My wife began running after Jackie died. She went on long runs to combat the pain.

The goal is to allow our feelings to be and not to resist, but instead, to move through them. Psychiatrist Carl Jung taught that whatever you resist persists. The more you resist anything in life, the more you bring it to you. Resisting feelings and avoiding potential pain brings more pain upon you. When we don't feel fully, we can't live fully. Our minds want to protect us from the pain and distress, but feelings must be felt.

Life is a series of peaks and valleys. When you are in the valley of grief, don't fight your emotions but acknowledge your reality and feel your feelings. It's messy and it's uncomfortable, but if you don't deal with your feelings, you will get stuck in your grief and in managing problematic behavior. Feelings are your friend, connect with them. Remember that God is with you in the peaks and valleys in life and will give you the courage to feel your feelings.

Embrace the Pain

Solomon wrote, "There is … a time to weep and a time to laugh, a time to mourn and a time to dance" (Ecclesiastes 3:1,4).

"Pain is a gift," according to Dr. Paul Brand, a British surgeon and author of *The Gift of Pain*: "Pain is one of God's great gifts to us."[2] That's the last thing grievers want to hear after their loss. Many people view pain as one of God's biggest mistakes. Prior to my loss, I never viewed pain as a gift, but I do now.

Pain is a gift because it demonstrates we have a capacity to feel. Pain informs us that we are still alive. What if we couldn't feel things in our body and soul? God created us with the ability to feel pain for a reason.

Dr. Brand's work with leprosy patients in India revealed that pain is an indicator that lets us know something is wrong; pain has a value that becomes clearest in its absence. Leprosy is a deadly disease because it keeps the nerves from informing the brain about the pain.

Pain is a gift that none of us want and yet none of us can do without. Pain is both an essential and unavoidable part of life. A key to navigating grief and loss is learning how to respond to pain.

We often seek to avoid our painful feelings or go underground with them and bury them.

Jesus Wept

Jesus was fully divine and fully human. He knew what it was like to feel his feelings and express his human emotions. His dear friend, Lazarus, died. Friends of the family were sitting Shiva with Lazarus' sisters, Mary, and Martha. If the grieving person wanted to talk, then you could converse. It's a way of saying, "I love you. I'm here for you. You're not alone." You might sit for hours or days: "When Jesus saw Mary weeping, and the Jews with her weeping, he was deeply moved in spirit and troubled" (John 11:33).

"'Where have you laid him?' he asked. 'Come and see, Lord,'" they replied (John 11:34).

"Jesus wept" (John 11:35).

Then, the Jews said, "See how he loved him!" (John 11:36). Jesus' tears were evidence of his love for Lazarus.

The shortest verse in the Bible is one of the most freeing verses in Scripture. Those two words, "Jesus wept," give us permission to weep in our sorrow because they reveal how Jesus modeled his grief. Grief is not a disease; it's a natural response to loss.

Jesus ends up raising Lazarus from the dead and yet he still weeps. His power does not rule out his grief. His ability to raise the dead doesn't rule out the pain and sorrow in his heart. He feels his feelings head on and weeps. You can have great faith in God and still weep. In fact, I believe spiritual maturity goes together with tears.

King David said, "I am worn out from sobbing. All night I flood my bed with weeping, drenching it with my tears" (Psalm 6:6). If there's one thing I've learned, it's that whatever you're feeling in that moment is okay. It's okay to feel anger, shock, denial, or fear. It's okay to have no answers, no explanations, and even no words.

In some religious traditions, there is a perception that weeping and mourning means that you doubt God, so people aren't encouraged to grieve. Please don't ever think it's more spiritual to hold in your tears.

I don't know how long ago you experienced your loss or if it was just last week, but I'm so sorry for your loss. Please don't avoid your feelings and think they will just go away. There is a high cost to holding onto your feelings. Loss brings pain and pain brings grief.

If you've never freely grieved, those feelings are still trapped somewhere inside. Allow yourself time to mourn and weep. If you try to hold in your tears and ignore your pain, there will be serious problems later. God gave us tears to shed in our grief, an outpouring of our inner pain. Jesus has power over life and death. He knows the beginning from the end. Jesus knew that a few minutes later, he would raise Lazarus from the dead and call him out of the tomb so that he would live again, and yet Jesus still weeps.

I think people all over the world would be well-served by watching Jesus weep. It might give them permission to weep and to fully grieve. Weeping is the language of the soul.

If the Son of God needs a good cry, then maybe so do I. And maybe so do you.

The Tears of Jesus

Poet Ann Weems suffered heartbreak when her twenty-one-year-old son, Todd, was murdered. She poured her grief into writing her own version of lament psalms. Here she writes a lament about the tears of Jesus.

> Jesus wept,
> and in his weeping,
> he joined himself forever to those who mourn.
> He stands now throughout all time,
> this Jesus weeping,
> with his arms about the weeping ones:
> "Blessed are those who mourn,
> for they shall be comforted."
> He stands with the mourners,
> for his name is God-with-us.
>
> Jesus wept.
> "Blessed are those who weep, for they shall be comforted."
> Someday.
> Someday God will wipe the tears from Rachel's eyes.
> in the godforsaken, obscene quicksand of life,
> there is a deafening alleluia,
> rising from the souls of those who weep,
> and of those who weep with those who weep.
> If you watch, you will see the hand of God,
> putting the stars back in their skies one by one.[3]

The Health Benefits of Tears

Crying is a phenomenon unique to humans, and is a natural response to emotions, from deep sadness and grief to extreme happiness and joy. In essence, tears are liquid emotions. Our bodies produce three kinds of tears: reflex, continuous, and emotional. Each kind has different healing roles.

Emotional tears have special health benefits and are especially relevant to us as grievers. Biochemist and tear expert, Dr. William Frey, discovered that emotional tears contain stress hormones that get flushed from your body through crying. Crying stimulates the production of endorphins, our body's natural painkiller and feel-good hormones. Bottom line, crying is good for you. It's healthy and it makes us feel better.[4]

Emotional tears heal your heart. Crying is essential to resolve grief when waves of tears regularly come over us after loss. Tears help us process the loss so we can keep living with open hearts. Otherwise, we are prone to depression.

While the eyes of all mammals are moistened and soothed by tears, only human beings shed tears in response to grief and sadness. God designed your body with the capacity to cry and provides health benefits with every tear, so feel your feelings and let the tears flow to help heal your heart and soul.

God Collects Our Tears in a Bottle

King David said, "You keep track of all my sorrows. You have collected all my tears in your bottle. You have recorded each one in your book" (Psalm 56:8 NLT). The idea behind keeping our tears in a bottle is remembrance. While God may not have a literal bottle filled with our tears (He may), He does remember every tear that falls from our eyes. This includes every tear we shed with the passing of a loved one or a significant loss. Our tears matter to God, and He remembers them all. The fact that God remembers my sorrow and tears brings me great comfort. I hope it does the same for you.

That being said, it's important to note that God does not merely collect tears. The tears of suffering humanity deeply move God. They call Him into action to restore that which has been lost, to rescue the brokenhearted, and to usher in a new creation. Tears are just temporary; someday, they will all be wiped away. Sadness will be turned into joy and mourning into dancing. Everything will be made new.

In the next chapter of *The School of Grief,* you will learn how to release your burden of guilt and regret, both of which often accompany grief.

CHAPTER 11:
TO RELEASE YOUR BURDEN OF GUILT

> *"Guilt is perhaps the most painful companion to death."*
> *Elisabeth Kubler Ros*

The third need of grievers is to release their burden of guilt and regret. Guilt accompanies grief in nearly every loss—it certainly did in mine. Regret, self-blame, and shame walk hand in hand with grief. The goal is to release the burden of guilt to get to the pure grief, so you can fully grieve.

Guilt and regret can be devastating after losing someone you love. The song, *Tears in Heaven*, by Eric Clapton may be the saddest song ever written about losing a loved one. Dealing with the loss of his four-year-old son, Conor, who fell from the 53rd floor of a building while playing tag with the housekeeper, the song helped Clapton come to terms with this tragedy and grieve the loss of his son.

The lyrics express his sadness and hopeful encounter with his son and what it would be like to see him in heaven. Clapton loved his son and expressed his desire to be a more involved parent to the mother of the child just a few days before his son's death. You can sense the uncertainty of his relationship with his son in the following lyric: "Would you know my name, if I saw you in heaven?"[1]

Guilt

Guilt is a powerful emotion. It can hold us in bondage, isolate us, and alter how we look at the world. Realistic guilt exists when we do something we know is wrong, but we may also unrealistically blame ourselves for things over which we had no control. Guilt causes us to punish ourselves and keeps us focused on the past.

Lynn Aubree Andrews was a life force. Her death came at the hands of a motorcycle accident, which took a large chunk of energy out of the world. Lynn was riding on the back of the bike when her fiancé accidentally hit a curb. Lynn flew off the bike and was killed instantly. Her fiancé lived. I facilitated the memorial service for the Andrews family as we celebrated Lynn's life. Her father, Mark, pulled me aside after our first meeting and told me to share that the family feels nobody is guilty of this tragedy and loss. I met her fiancé at the memorial. He was extremely broken and sorrowful. He survived and she didn't.

Guilt is frequently an emotion associated with the loss of a loved one: "If only I had done this or that." This was an accident. Nobody was to blame. This is what I shared at the memorial: "Our church is a no guilt zone. Rather, we offer hope, not condemnation. We all feel a tremendous sorrow but hopefully, we can let go of any guilt or regret." Mark, his wife, and his other daughter maintained their relationship with Lynn's fiancé and continue to support him in his life endeavors.

Feelings That Accompany Grief

There are many feelings that accompany the experience of grief, but few are more difficult to understand than the feelings of guilt and regret. Guilt and regret are painful feelings that often arise as a follow up to other feelings. A person might feel relieved that their loved one is no longer suffering, then experience guilt about feeling relieved. Someone might feel anger about circumstances related to a death, then feel guilty about feeling angry. Guilt often accompanies other grief-related feelings. This is one reason it is so difficult to understand.

Guilt may be a form of self-criticism for not meeting your own expectations and standards, and it may arise when you're grieving a significant loss. Holding yourself responsible for thoughts or perceived shortcomings can add the burden of guilt and regret to your grieving process.

Guilt is a feeling that may come from believing you didn't say enough, do enough, or make enough of an effort when you had the opportunity. After your loss, you might start to blame yourself for an outcome that wasn't really within your control. For instance, many women blame themselves for a miscarriage. The truth is most miscarriages are outside your control. Try not to add to your grief by blaming yourself.

Guilt is not logical, but it can serve a purpose in our minds because our minds want to make sense of a death or loss. This is why guilt often comes in many forms. That being said, it can be more comfortable to feel guilty than helpless. It can point to a primal wound that we have experienced in the past.

Guilt keeps us from being able to be present where we are. It's a way for us to have the illusion of control and reinforces long-held beliefs we may have about ourselves.

Unfortunately, we tend to be too hard on ourselves. Our minds can be cruel to us in grief. We would never talk to others in the same harsh tone that we use to talk to ourselves. Please be kind and forgiving toward yourself in your pain.

Remember What You Did Right

We all make mistakes. Healthy amounts of guilt and regret can inspire us to become better people and make us more compassionate toward others in pain. Be a light in a dark world.

Allow yourself to remember what you did right. Guilt and regret are feelings that focus on what may have gone wrong. Acknowledge those feelings but remember to look at the bigger picture. In Jackie's case, the big picture was that she had a great childhood, a wonderful family, many friends, a fairy tale existence, albeit was only for five years. She died a merciful death with little to no physical pain or suffering. About a thousand people came to her memorial service to show their love for her and our family.

Focus on the good memories, not the bad. Maybe we could have handled the radiation dilemma differently or maybe we should have questioned the doctors some more. The bottom line is we made tremendous memories with Jackie, though short-lived. She rode on the back of my motorcycle with me in our gated community. She loved when I sang songs to her or wrestled with her. She loved to swim in a pool, the American river, or the ocean. She loved church and her friends. I had the privilege of praying with her when she accepted

Christ as her Savior. These are unforgettable memories I will always cherish.

Survivor Guilt

A common feeling among parents who have lost a child is survivor guilt, as we believe children are supposed to outlive their parents, not the other way around. Most parents feel as though they have failed as parents and question their abilities. The role of being a provider, protector, and mentor to that child diminishes after the death of the child, creating a confusion of identity, which can be even stronger in parents who only had that one child.

When parents lose a child, they also tend to lose social supports that were previously available to them. This loss of support often comes from the loss of interaction with other parents, as these parents may avoid interacting with them. This is usually because they are unsure of what to say to the parents who have lost a child, and don't want to even entertain that this situation could happen to them.

Experiencing guilt when grieving may have major mental health implications. A recent study by the University of Groningen called *Grief in Bereavement* found that guilt was directly associated with a higher chance of experiencing complicated grief and depression. Complicated grief is often referred to as prolonged grief disorder and is diagnosed when symptoms of grief persist for more than 12 months after the loss.

Signs of Guilt During Grief

How guilt during grief presents itself in daily life. Common behaviors may include:

- denying yourself basic care
- avoiding potentially joyful connections or comfort
- substance abuse
- putting yourself in situations that may put your safety in jeopardy

Guilt Can Also Emerge From:

- social isolation
- avoiding topics, places, or people
- getting irritated with yourself
- engaging in negative self-talk
- self-sabotage[2]

Regret

Regret is what we feel when we identify the "shoulda, woulda, couldas," things that we would have done differently if we had known then what we know now. For instance, we may find ourselves wishing we had spent more time with a loved one before death, wishing we had said "I love you" more often, or wondering whether a different course of treatment could have possibly changed the outcome.

We All Have Choices

You and I have choices about the kinds of people we are going to become after our loss. We have a choice as to whether we're going to become bitter or not. Why is it so easy to become bitter when we lose someone we love?

A Woman Named Naomi

There is a woman in the book of Ruth named Naomi. She loses her husband and two sons and is left with her two daughters-in-law: Ruth and Orpah. When they move to a new town, she tells the people there not to call her Naomi anymore and to call her Mara instead, which means bitter in Hebrew. (Ruth 1:20).

Job's Wife

Job's faith was greatly tested. He lost everything and was covered in boils but never became bitter. His wife, on the other hand, was consumed with bitterness. At one point, she basically said to him "Why are you still trying to maintain your integrity? Why don't you just curse God and die" (Job 2:9).

Have you chosen to become bitter because of your loss?

Maybe you're feeling the guilt that often accompanies loss. "If only I would've done something differently." We can become racked with guilt until it eventually seeps into our mind and body, making itself a part of our identity. Usually, we aren't even aware that this is happening. But if you are, don't let it happen.

Is guilt keeping your heart from healing?

Accept God's Forgiveness

There are two kinds of guilt: false and real. If you've done something wrong, repent and ask God to forgive you. Accept God's forgiveness, forgive others, and free yourself from guilt. Apologize from your heart in prayer and let all negative thoughts go: "Repent, then, and turn to God, so that your sins may be wiped out, that times of refreshing may come from the Lord" (Acts 3:19).

No relationship is perfect. We have all made mistakes. There are things you wanted to do with your loved one, or things you wish you didn't say. Thinking about all the things that could have

been different can overwhelm you. Paul wrote, "Therefore, there is now no condemnation for those who are in Christ Jesus" (Romans 8:1).

Without Christ's forgiveness, you will live with guilt and shame. The apostle Peter wrote, "At one time you did not know God's mercy, but now you have received his mercy" (1 Peter 2:10 GNT). What happens when you receive God's mercy? He wipes out your sins. It's as if all your sins are written on a whiteboard and He takes a giant eraser and wipes them all away.

It's called grace.

Four Ways That God Forgives Us:

Freely

"He (God) will have mercy on them, and to our God, for he will freely pardon" (Isaiah 55:7 NIV).

Instantly

"If we confess our sins, he is faithful and just and will forgive us our sins and purify us from all unrighteousness" (1 John 1:9).

Completely

"(God) forgives all your sins and heals all your diseases… For as high as the heavens are above the earth, so great is his love for those who fear him; as far as the east is from the west, so far has he removed our transgressions from us" (Psalm 103:3,11-12).

Continually

"You will again have compassion on us; you will tread our sins underfoot and hurl all our iniquities into the depths of the sea" (Micah 7:19).

Corrie ten Boom said, "God buries our sins in the depths of the sea and then puts up a sign that reads, 'No fishing.'"

Confidence in God's Forgiveness

Here are two reasons you can be confident that God has totally and completely forgiven you:

God's nature is to forgive: "I am the God who forgives your sins, and I do this because of who I am. I will not hold your sins against you" (Isaiah 43:25 GNT).

Jesus has paid for all your sins. Paul wrote, "For by the blood of Christ we are set free" (Ephesians 1:7 GNT). God forgives you—not because you've somehow earned forgiveness but because Jesus has already done the work to make forgiveness possible. Jesus' death on the cross paid for every sin you've ever committed and ever will commit. God is merciful and has forgiven you.

Will you forgive yourself?

A Tragic Accident

Ron and Sue were members of a church I pastored in Southern California. They had a home with a pool in the backyard. The pool had a small fence around it with a locked door at the entrance. They were watching the grandkids while their daughter and her husband were away for the weekend. Somehow, one of the toddlers got loose, went down by the pool, and made his way into the water. They found him minutes later at the bottom of the pool. They tried to revive him and called 911 immediately. The paramedics came quickly and tried to bring him back, but he was gone. He had drowned and the grandparents were in shock, completely devastated. They had the unbearable task of having to call their daughter and son-in-law to tell them their son was dead.

Sue wrote me a letter a year after the accident. I talked about forgiveness the previous Sunday and the importance of forgiving yourself as God has forgiven you. Sue shared that she was finally able to forgive herself as she shed buckets of tears of thanks to God for her newfound freedom from blame, shame, self-loathing, and unforgiveness.

When you forgive, you heal. When you let go, you grow. Desmond Tutu said, "Forgiveness says you are given another chance to make a new beginning." Forgiveness doesn't change your past but it sure can change your future.

I'm so happy Sue and Ron were able to forgive themselves and live.

In the next chapter of *The School of Grief*, you will learn how to face your fears on your grief journey.

CHAPTER 12:
TO FACE YOUR FEARS

> *"No one ever told me that grief felt so much like fear."*
> *C.S. Lewis*

Grief Feels Like Fear

The fourth need for grievers is to face their fears. Grief feels like fear because fear, in a sense, becomes our reality. Our worst nightmare came true when our daughter died.

Healthy Fear and Unhealthy Fear

Fear can be healthy and unhealthy. It is programmed into our nervous systems and gives us the survival instincts we need to keep ourselves safe from danger. Primal fears help us survive. A lion in the bush should be feared. Stoves are hot and knives are sharp.

That being said, fear is unhealthy when it makes you more cautious than you need to be to stay safe. Fear is unhealthy when it prevents you from moving forward in your grief, therefore holding you back from any progress or steps forward. The goal is not to necessarily eliminate fear but to integrate it.

Types of Fear Accompanied by Grief:
- Fear of it happening again
- Fear of being abandoned by God and loved ones
- Fear of not grieving correctly
- Fear of vulnerability
- Fear of never being happy again
- Fear of the unknown
- Fear of change
- Fear of death

Perfect Love Drives Out Fear

Fear is an emotion caused by the belief that something or someone poses a threat to us or our loved ones. The Devil uses unhealthy fear as a weapon to disrupt our faith. He wants us to doubt God and His plan for us. If Satan can move us to a point of unbelief, then he can cause us to distrust God.

The Bible says that fear doesn't come from God: "There is no fear in love. But perfect love drives out fear" (1 John 4:18). It also says, "God is love" (1 John 4:16). When you're afraid, it's not from God because the essence of God is love and there is no fear in God's love.

As a pastor, I've learned the number one thing most people fear is death—either your own death or the death of a loved one. The Devil will use that fear to manipulate you. But the good news is Jesus defeated death and destroyed the Devil's work. So, now, when we grieve, we grieve with hope.

We grieve because we miss our loved ones who have gone on before us. We fully grieve but know we will see them again in heaven.

Whenever you sense fear creeping into your psyche—whether it's the fear of your own death, the death of a loved one. or some other fear—remember that unhealthy fear is not from God. Ask Him to help you face your fears and to drive out your fears with His perfect love.

Facing My Fear

After Jackie died, I took two weeks off from work, which was not nearly enough time to process the pain of her loss but there was some conflict at church I needed to come back to deal with. When I returned to work, I took a short detour each day to the church, so I wouldn't pass by the radiation center where we had such a horrific experience with Jackie. Jackie's radiation treatment left a bad taste in my mouth, and I had a bad memory of the place and that day. The center had become a trigger for the pain and anger I felt regarding Jackie's brain tumor. On the day of treatment, Jackie cried for a few hours and didn't understand why she had to go through such an agonizing procedure.

After a couple of weeks of avoiding the Auburn Radiation Oncology Center, I felt ready to face my fear head on. I drove up Bell Road and came face-to-face with the radiation center. I parked on the side of the road and walked straight to the front, staring that place down for a few minutes as I prayed to God for strength to overcome my fear.

A few minutes later, I drove the extra two blocks to work. After embracing my feelings and standing up to the fear, I never took that detour to work again.

The secret to eliminating fear in your life is to move against the fear. King David said, "Yeah, though I walk through the valley of the shadow of death. I will fear no evil for Thou art with me" (Psalm 23:4 KJV). If God is for us, who can be against us? When you are ready in your grief process, do the very thing you fear.

Navigating the rocky terrain of grief is a faith journey. David said, "The LORD is my light, and my salvation, whom shall I fear. The LORD is the stronghold of my life – of whom shall I be afraid" (Psalm 27:1-2).

Physical Symptoms Can Accompany Grief

Grieving people feel anxious about their own health and the safety of their loved ones. Anxiety causes fear, which can then manifest physically. One week after Jackie died, my other daughter, Jessica, who was seven years old at the time, was experiencing terrible pain in her abdomen. Carrie and I thought, *Oh no, not again!* She would bend over in pain from stomach cramps and cry because the pain was so intense. We took her to the hospital immediately—the same one Jackie received treatment at—to determine what was wrong.

After a battery of tests, the doctor said, "Mr. and Mrs. Page, there is nothing physically wrong with your daughter. It was all in her head, which caused her to have pain in her stomach." Jessica was having a difficult time processing the hurt and pain from losing her sister. If you swallow your emotions, your stomach keeps score. This is what Jessica was experiencing after the loss. The pain got worse at night. This was when she would normally spend time with Jackie, talking themselves to sleep every night in a bedroom they shared together. After a couple of weeks, the stomach pain went away.

What We Run from Pursues Us and What We Face Transforms Us

What we resist, persists. What we run from pursues us. What we face transforms us. The transformation is found in the rubble of our grief and pain.

It's natural to want to run away from pain and disconnect from it. We are biologically predisposed to avoid pain. Contrary to what some people believe, intense pain from grief is not like touching a hot stove. When you're in intense grief, it's like the entire hot stove has fallen on you. No wonder we want to avoid those feelings.

We must honor the pace of our grief. We will continually revisit grief throughout our life. Grief lasts longer than we think. Grief never ends because our love never ends. I never got to experience Jackie's graduation from high school. I never got to teacher her how to drive. I never got to walk her down the aisle for her wedding. I never got to experience the birth of her child and my grandchild. I never dreamed we'd experience grief in such a profound way at Jessica's wedding as Jackie was Jessica's maid of honor. This was extremely gratifying for me but at the same time, it was incredibly painful.

As human beings, we can't take all the pain in one day. We touch the pain (hot stove) and then retreat and need a break. Respect the wisdom and timing of your grief process. I've learned that it's not my job to move people along quickly in their grief. They need to go at their own pace.

Buffaloes Run into the Storm

Grief is a storm in our lives—maybe the biggest storm we'll ever face. The only choice that we have is how we respond to the storm. And more specifically, when and how we respond to those storms.

Colorado is known for the world-famous Rocky Mountains. Many people don't realize that the state of Colorado is divided nearly in half: the western part of the state is the great Rocky Mountains and to the eastern part of the state is the great Kansas Plains. Because of this unique landscape, they have the Rocky Mountains and the Plains. Colorado is one of the only places in the world that has both buffaloes and cows.

When storms come, they nearly always come from the West and roll out towards the East. Cows can sense that a storm is coming from the West. So, a cow will try to run East to get away from the storm. The only problem is cows aren't very fast. So, the storm catches up with them rather quickly. Without knowing any better, the cows continue to try to outrun the storm. But instead of outrunning the storm, they run with the storm, maximizing the amount of pain, time, and frustration they experience. We, as human beings, do the same with the storms in our lives, including loss and grief.

What buffaloes do is unique in the animal kingdom. Buffaloes wait for the storm to cross right over the crest of the peak of the mountaintop. And as the storm rolls over the ridge, buffaloes turn and charge directly West into the storm. They run at the storm and by doing so, they run straight through it, minimizing the amount of pain, time, and frustration they experience from that storm. This is a great metaphor for all of us who have experienced loss because even though our losses are different, we all face storms.[1]

We don't get to choose whether we experience storms. The only choice that we have is *how* we respond to the storms in our lives. Which direction are you heading?

Chasing Daylight or Running Toward the Darkness?

Poet John Donne makes a point that although east and west seem the farthest removed on a map, they eventually meet on a globe. What therefore appear as opposites come together in time if we follow one or the other long enough and far enough.

Jerry Sittser wrote, "The quickest way for anyone to reach the sun and the light of day is not to run west, chasing after the setting sun, but to head east, plunging into the darkness until one comes to the sunrise."[2]

We have the power to choose the direction our lives will head; will we run from our loss or face it the best we are able? Darkness from grief is inevitable and unavoidable, so maybe it would be best to walk into the darkness rather than try to outrun it. Maybe it would be best to allow my experience of loss to take me on a journey wherever that may lead, and to allow myself to be transformed by my suffering rather than to think I can somehow avoid it. It's your choice in terms of which way you turn.

In the next chapter of *The School of Grief*, you will learn that grief is not something we get over. Loss is something we learn to live with and can serve as a wake-up call to live life to the fullest.

CHAPTER 13:
TO NOT GET OVER IT – BUT GROW INTO IT.

> *"Grief isn't something to get over."*
> Mary Lamia

Grief Isn't Something We Get Over

Grief is a tool God gives us to get through our losses and transitions in life. We tend to use the phrase "getting over something." This mistaken notion that grief is something you work through, finish, and get over is hurting rather than helping those in grief. Feelings of grief and sadness are common for many years. In fact, sometimes they are common for a lifetime after the actual death occurred.

I haven't gotten over Jackie's loss; instead, her loss became a part of who I am. She is a large part of my story on earth and something I'm very proud of. Jackie has become part of the landscape of my life.

TO NOT GET OVER IT – BUT GROW INTO IT.

Grief isn't something you get over. It's not over; it's into. It's not through; it's absorbing your loved one into your life. Sittser wrote, "I did not get over the loss of my loved ones; rather, I absorbed the loss into my life, like soil receives decaying matter, until it became a part of who I am."[1] Jackie has become part of the fabric of my life and who I am as a person.

We will carry our losses for the rest of our lives. There is no stage called closure in grief, although our friends and family may want us to find closure because our pain makes them uncomfortable.

Your Loss Does Not Define You

Your loss does not define your identity, rather the defining factor will be how you respond to your loss. One of the lessons I learned through my daughter's death is that I can't control everything that happens in my life. The key isn't what happens to you but how you respond to what happens to you. I believe that 10% of life is what happens to us and 90% is how we respond.

Viktor Frankl was an Austrian psychiatrist and a Holocaust survivor. While a prisoner in a Nazi death camp in Auschwitz in World War II, he was stripped of everything in his possession, including his gold wedding band. As he stood there naked in front of the German guards, he realized they could take everything from him except his power to choose. He wrote, "Everything can be taken from a man but one thing: the last of the human freedoms – to choose one's attitude in any given set of circumstances, to choose one's own way."[2] Frankl refused to yield ultimate power to his captors and circumstances.

In the same way, I decided my life was not going to be defined by my daughter's death, even though I was commonly known as "the pastor who lost his daughter" throughout the city of Auburn. Instead, my life would be defined by my response to my daughter's death.

Honestly, after two decades, I am still bewildered by my daughter's death. I don't know why she got a brain tumor, and I don't understand why she had to die. I've just decided to just keep on living after my loss and trust God to bring good out of the mess, to create beauty out of the ashes. As God began healing my heart, I was able to come alongside others and help them with their grief. My life was not defined by her loss but strengthened by it.

God Designed Our Hearts to Grieve

God designed our hearts to grieve. It's one of its main functions and purposes. Grieving is a necessary and ongoing practice to help us live and adapt to a turbulent world filled with heartache and pain. What a tremendous gift from God to our heart, body, and soul, to allow it to fulfill its most beautiful and noble purpose. Grieving helps us process the tragedies of the human experience and experience the comfort of God in the process. Grief, when tended to well, tends to our hearts well, which allows us to care for the hearts of others.

The Heart Enlarges

The heart doesn't break; it enlarges. The heart is elastic, like a balloon and can expand, stretch, and grow. As a result, we can increase the capacity of our souls and become more compassionate, empathetic, and loving as people. Grieving is love, and love is grieving. Grief and love are two sides of the same heart. You grieve because you love. Without love, there is no grief. I believe because of my loss and because of your loss, we have a greater capacity for love and joy. And I believe we can accomplish things in the future that we never dreamed possible.

Growing Larger Through Loss

The death of a loved one can serve as a wake-up call to live life to the fullest. Death reminds us of how precious life is and what we could do if we had the courage to seize the day. Experiencing loss is an opportunity to grow by taking responsibility for your own life and making sure you don't waste it.

Thus, it's not true that we become less through loss unless we allow it to crush us and become bitter. On the contrary, loss can make us more. One of the grief myths is that our grief gets smaller over time and that becomes the goal. The goal isn't to make our grief smaller. It's for us to become bigger and to grow around our grief. Grief won't get smaller, but you will get bigger.

As a result, you become *resilient*. This growth process does much more than restore you to who you once were prior to your loss. Rather, you emerge from the experience transformed into a truer expression of who you were really meant to be. I keep asking, "How can I grow through this? How can I grow in my faith? How can I be better at walking alongside others in their grief?"

Author and radio host, Joni Eareckson Tada, became a quadriplegic as a result of a diving accident when she was seventeen years old and has been paralyzed from the shoulders down since. One of her mantras is, "Lean into the pain, grow from the pain."[3] Our natural reaction to pain is to say, "No,

I want to get rid of the pain." We spend much of our time trying to avoid pain and loss and the call of discipleship is to grow into them. Growing larger through loss is a process. To grow you must lean into the pain. Don't rush the process.

Post Traumatic Growth

German philosopher, Friedrich Nietzsche, said, "That which does not kill us, makes us stronger." I believe this is generally true. We hear a lot about Post Traumatic Stress Disorder (PTSD), but Post Traumatic Growth (PTG) occurs more often. Studies show that some trauma survivors report positive changes and enhanced personal development after experiencing their trauma. PTG refers to any beneficial change resulting from a major life crisis or traumatic event. That being said, PTG does not lessen grief. So, don't look at it as an end point to your pain. Rather, PTG co-exists with our distress and is something that only exists because of our distress and our attempt to cope. Like much of grief, PTG is unexpected, but can be a beautiful byproduct of pain.

Many people with PTG experience a positive shift by having a renewed appreciation for life in which they adopt a new worldview with new possibilities for themselves, feel more personal strength, experience improved relationships, and feel increasingly satisfied on a spiritual level.

How Long Will I Grieve?

How long will your loved one be dead? Because if they're going to be dead for a long time then you're going to grieve for a long time. But that doesn't mean you'll always grieve with pain. People are afraid that healing means forgetting their loved ones or what happened to them. It's not forgetting them but rather it's remembering them with love, talking about them, and keeping the connection with them alive. Kessler said, "Healing is remembering your loved one with more love than pain."

Will I Ever Recover?

Regarding recovery from loss, there is a difference between a broken leg and an amputation. We can't go back to something else before. I believe there are experiences in life where there is no recovery—if by recovery we mean we're going to be able to go back to something we had before. When it came to my loss, I had to change my definition of recovery. If we mean complete recover and healing in this life, then I have not recovered and don't think I ever will until I get on the other side of heaven.

Authors John James and Russell Friedman in their book, *The Grief Recovery Handbook*, define recovery as "Feeling better... claiming your circumstances instead of your circumstances claiming you and your happiness... finding new meaning for living, without fear of being hurt again... being able to enjoy fond memories without having them precipitate painful feelings of regret or remorse... acknowledging that it is perfectly all right to feel sad from time to time and to talk about those feelings no matter how those around you react ...being able to forgive others when they say or do things that you know are based on their lack of knowledge about grief... one day realizing that your ability to talk about the loss you've experienced is indeed normal and healthy."[4]

Based on the above definition, I believe I'm recovering well. It's taken a long time and a lot of work to get to where I am now. And yet, I still miss Jackie greatly, talk about her all the time, and hold onto the hope that I will see her again in heaven. But I don't feel guilty anymore for feeling good! Feeling good is not disrespectful to her memory.

Railroad Tracks

Does God want us to be continually sad? No. I used to think life was a series of peaks and valleys; sometimes we're up, then we're down. But I've come to realize that life is much more like a set of parallel train tracks, with joy and sorrow running inseparably throughout our days.

Every day of your life, good things happen. Beauty, accomplishment, and pleasure. That's the track of joy. But every day of your life also holds disappointment, struggles, and losses. That's the track of sorrow. Joy and sorrow will always be present together.

Kay Warren, in her book *Choose Joy*, writes, "One of our toughest challenges in life is to learn how to live on both of those tracks at the same time. But there's hope! Consider what it's like to stand between two sets of train tracks and look off into the horizon. Those parallel tracks come together as we look ahead. They are no longer distinguishable as two separate tracks.

"That's the way it will be for us too. During our lifetime, we stand on the tracks looking for signs of Jesus Christ's return. We watch for the sights and sounds that will alert us that his appearance is very close. One day, in the brightness of his coming, we will meet him face to face. And when we do, the tracks of joy and sorrow will merge. The sorrow will disappear forever, and only the joy will remain."

Love Never Dies

Love always survives death. Let's not give death any more power than it already has. Death can end a physical life but not our relationship with our loved one, and certainly not our love because love always survives death. It never ends.

In the next chapter of *The School of Grief*, you will learn about the process of turning your pain into purpose, which helps heal your heart and guide others on their grief journey.

CHAPTER 14:
TO TURN YOUR PAIN INTO PURPOSE

> *"God never wastes a hurt! Pain can point you to your purpose. Your greatest ministry will likely come out of your deepest pain."*
> Rick Warren

Finding meaning and turning your pain into purpose is the sixth need we all have after our loss. It doesn't happen on the first day after your loss but happens over time. Before you turn your pain into purpose, you must acknowledge, accept, and grieve your loss. Know that God can take the most painful experience in your life and use it for good.

Gloves for Grief

I discussed Terra and Brian Pickett who lost their son, Weston, in a previous chapter. Eighteen months after the loss, Terra founded a nonprofit to help others in their grief. Terra realized that grief was not meant to be carried alone but was meant to be shared. She began her healing in a support group at Saddleback Church called Empty Arms for women who have lost children. Through the group, she met Ashley Guarrasi, a boxing instructor and Nike trainer. Ashley, like Terra, had also lost a son named Zane. The two women connected in their pain and together, they founded Gloves for Grief. Their motto is "Punching our pain into purpose."

They hold action-packed events all over Southern California that include training by Guarrasi on shadowboxing and bag work followed by a time of cool down, stretching, and breathing. Those who attend enjoy live music, connection, and community. They address the mind, body, and soul of grievers. Movement and fitness provide a healthy physical release for grief where no words are needed. I recently participated in one of their events and found it very soothing to hit the boxing bag. One woman remarked, "Sometimes it just feels good to hit something." I found this to be true. Terra and Ashley turned their pain into purpose.

The Power of Meaning

Loss is what happens to you; meaning is what you make happen. Meaning reflects the love we have for those we have lost. Finding meaning is often where our healing resides. Finding meaning is the key to finding purpose and joy after loss. I encourage counselors who work with grieving people to help them search for meaning in their loss.

Meaning is relative and personal. It takes time. It usually doesn't appear right away but builds up over the years. Meaning doesn't have to be grand or dramatic. You don't have to start a nonprofit company to find meaning but you do have to grieve your loss prior to finding meaning.

Meaning doesn't equal understanding why your loved one died. You may never understand the reason for your loss. I've reframed my question, changing it from "Why did my daughter die?" to "Why did I live? Why am I still here?" So, what are you still here?

How to Discern Your Purpose

Leadership author, John Maxwell, asks three questions when he wants to really get to know someone. People's answers to these questions give him great insight into their heart. I believe these three questions can help us in discerning our purpose after our loss. The questions are: What do you cry about? What do you dream about? What do you sing about?[1]

The first question answers what will bring you fulfillment tomorrow. It deals with your own pain and considers a way of turning that pain into a purpose that could bless others. The last two questions speak to what touches you at a deep level today.

The answers to these questions can often help people discover their passion and purpose. We need to know our passion to discover our purpose. For me, helping grieving people after their loss is what I cry, dream, and sing about. It brings me great satisfaction and fulfillment. You will want to consider answering these three questions yourself to turn your pain into purpose.

My Mess Became My Ministry

Pain can point you to your purpose in life. Our deepest life messages come out of our deepest pain. My mess became my ministry. My misery became my message. My pain became my purpose. I didn't choose to go into grief ministry; it chose me. But I love what I do. I get to come alongside people in their darkest hour and bring comfort and hope. Nearly every

TO TURN YOUR PAIN INTO PURPOSE

day, I talk to somebody about loss and grief in my role as a care pastor.

A few years after Jackie died, I was asked to speak at Forest Lawn Mortuaries 100-Year Anniversary. I spoke about purpose. Then, they asked if I would do funerals for them and trained me to become a certified funeral celebrant. I conducted celebrant and clergy funeral services for Forest Lawn for over five years. They also asked me to speak at a number of their Holiday Candle Lighting Memorial Services to remember those who died. It's a service to honor a loved one's memory and celebrate all that that person did to light up their life and the lives of everyone they touched. I spoke at these events in different cities as we saw thousands of people attend who were looking for hope.

March 4th used to be the worst day of the year for me. But I decided to be intentional and to turn my pain into purpose by shooting a hundred free throws on that day to raise money for the HEART Ministry in Kenya, Africa, to save lives. I call it *Hoops into Hope*. I've raised over $10,000 over the years for this significant ministry.

My life is not defined by my daughter's death but inspired by her life. Her death transformed my life. Now, instead of being tortured each year by the memory of her death, I now view it as a day of hope to help others in her honor.

Jackie loved to dance and was part of the *Pamelot School of Dance* in Auburn, CA. Pamelot was founded by Pam Harrold. Jackie was learning ballet, tap, and jazz. After her death, Pam created a dance scholarship in Jackie's name, which is given to one young girl dancer each year. A year after Jackie's passing, we attended a dance recital where Pam presented a young girl with the first Jackie Page Dance Scholarship. We feel so honored that Pam and the Pamelot Family witnessed our grief, honored our little girl, and are keeping Jackie's memory alive.

This past spring, I had the privilege of baptizing Terra Pickett on March 26th, which, the year before, had been the worst day of her life as it was the day Weston passed. Terra figured if she still has air in her lungs, then her story isn't over. She decided to create another memory that was equally life changing. Terra said, "I never knew God was all I needed, until He was all I had. This past year, my faith has kept me breathing. I want to commit the rest of my life to God.

March 26th will always be the worst day of my life, but now it will also be shared with a day filled with hope." Baptism symbolizes the death of Jesus on a cross for our sins, his burial, and his resurrection. It's a symbol of new life and now Terra will always remember this day with hope.

I turned my pain into purpose by starting our Hope for Grief Community at Saddleback Church. It's become a central gathering for grievers. Our relationship with our loved ones has shifted from one of physical presence to one of memory—a spiritual presence. Our Grief Community seeks to keep that memory alive and to honor our loved ones by sharing lessons we've learned and are still learning from them. I enjoy organizing and teaching at this unique event. I train staff members and volunteers to help others with grief. We talk about our loved ones. This is a safe place to do that. It's a time to remember the past, live in the present, and trust that the future is going to be good because God is good. Attending our grief community lets everyone know they are not alone in their grief.

A young girl named Jesse Rees had joy, hope, and peace amid her own cancer diagnosis and visited other kids with cancer in the hospital, giving out JoyJars—jars stuffed with toys, games, and activities for kids fighting cancer—that she created. Erik Rees, her father, started NEGU (Never Ever Give Up) to honor his 12-year-old daughter, who died of cancer. Their mission is to encourage every kid fighting cancer to never ever give up. The Jesse Rees Foundation gave out over 425,000 JoyJars and raised over 32 million dollars in their first 10 years to help kids fight cancer.

Kay Warren, out of her own pain over the loss of her son, started a Mental Health Community at Saddleback. Most recently, Kay started a yearly event called *Belle Donne*, which means *beautiful women* in Italian. Mother's Day is a time to celebrate the beautiful women in our lives. It can also leave women who have experienced grief and loss around motherhood feeling less than beautiful. A mother's grief can create a complicated holiday for many women. I've had the privilege of leading this ministry with the goal of providing a sacred space to honor a mother's grief.

Tina Burke, a friend and member of our Hope for Grief Community, suffered the loss of her 21-year-old son, Christian, when he accidentally overdosed on drugs laced with fentanyl. Tina was devastated. I applaud Tina for turning her pain into purpose by advocating against drug deaths by fentanyl, which has become an epidemic in our country. Tina is passionate about educating others about this horrific drug to save lives.

Redemptive Suffering

Redemptive suffering is the practice of taking our pain and allowing God to transform it into a way to help others. Suffering has great value if it is consecrated to God for the sake of serving others. Redemptive suffering is using your pain to help other people in their pain. It unleashes the love of Jesus and brings comfort to a hurting world. This is the key to turning pain into purpose.

Paul said, "Praise be to the God and Father of our Lord Jesus Christ, the Father of compassion and the God of all comfort, who comforts us in all our troubles, so that we can comfort those in any trouble with the comfort we ourselves receive from God" (2 Corinthians 1:3-4 NIV).

God is "the Father of Compassion." The Greek word translated as compassion means "deep feeling about someone's pain or misfortune." That's how God the Father feels about you. He's also "the God of All Comfort." When our hearts are breaking, when we are overwhelmed with grief, God's comfort becomes a healing ointment to our souls. He comforts us with the truth of His love, presence, and amazing grace.

Doesn't Waste Your Pain

God doesn't want to waste your hurt; he wants to recycle your pain to help others. He will recycle your pain for someone else's gain. God comforts us for a specific reason, "So that we can comfort those in any trouble with the comfort we ourselves receive from God." Our Heavenly Father wants us to do something in response to the comfort He has given to us. God expects us to use our pain to help others.

God uses our pain to make us more sensitive to other people's pain. Pain makes you more empathetic to those who are experiencing the same kind of pain you are. Rather than focusing on your pain, you can channel it to help others in their pain.

God Wants to Redeem Your Suffering

Who is better qualified to minister to a parent grieving the loss of a child than another parent who has experienced such grief? Who is better qualified to help someone with an addiction than someone who has battled addiction? Who is better qualified to walk with someone through a cancer diagnosis than someone who has fought cancer?

Think of your greatest loss, the most painful situation you've ever faced. God doesn't want you to waste that hurt; rather, He wants to redeem your suffering and use you to serve others.

The Model of Jesus

The cross of Jesus Christ reveals the love of God for humanity and his willingness to die in our place to take our sins upon himself. His pain truly was our gain. He turned the greatest adversity the world has ever known into the greatest advantage. Jesus' death on the cross gives meaning to suffering. He "did not come to suppress suffering all at once, nor to explain it, nor to justify it. He came to assume it and to transform it."[2] We can only understand the meaning of suffering by recognizing God's great love, as he gave up His only Son so that we could be forgiven and have eternal life.

The Art of Kintsugi

Kintsugi is a Japanese philosophy, art, and practice that treats breakage and repair as part of the history of an object, rather than something to disguise. Broken pottery is repaired using a lacquer containing gold powder. Instead of attempting to hide the repair, Kintsugi illuminates it. This art form is driven by a deep desire to restore and rebuild, giving new life to something precious that had been broken. It's a great metaphor for healing from loss; God's restoration process.

The result is a mended heart, which pays honor to our Redeemer, history, and story. What was broken has now been restored into something valuable and beautiful.

God is in the process of redeeming our stories. Redemption looks to the future but does not erase the past. Jesus bears the scars on his hands on his resurrected body. God promises to redeem our lives by mending what is broken, healing what is sick, and righting what is wrong. This incredible story of redemption is based on the work of Jesus, who came into this world to make us new, which he accomplished through his life, death on a cross, and resurrection.

Jackie Power

One of the most thrilling experiences in my life came one ordinary morning. Jackie's tumor was progressing each day. Malignant brain tumors normally grow quickly and spread into other brain tissue. When a tumor grows into or presses on an area of the brain, it may stop that part of the brain from working the way it should. Brain tumors are like roots of a tree. They can grow vertically or horizontally, in whatever direction they choose. Jackie was losing her motor skills.

She went from running everywhere to walking and then to crawling. She was at a point where she couldn't even crawl anymore. She lost her ability to speak but was able to make sounds, like grunts. We developed a communication system with her so that when she wanted to go somewhere in the house, she would make a certain sound, we'd pick her up, and she would point to where she wanted to go.

TO TURN YOUR PAIN INTO PURPOSE

On this occasion, I picked her up and she pointed toward the kitchen. I carried her to the kitchen, and she motioned for me to set her down on the kitchen counter. I figured she wanted something to eat so I picked her up and carried her toward the fridge.

She motioned for me to set her down on the counter. I realized she wasn't hungry. She used to climb up on the counter, ask me to back up, and then take a flying leap into my arms. To me, Jackie was *The Celebrated Jumping Frog of Calaveras County*. She reached a point where she was leaping nearly four feet across the kitchen into my arms.

I couldn't believe what happened next.

She tried to stand, using every ounce of strength and every fiber in her little body. Looking like a fawn attempting to stand for the first time, her little legs wobbled as she willed her way into a crouched position, finally standing completely upright.

Before the tumor, I would stand a foot away from the counter and she would hold up her right hand and motion for me to move back. Each time she gave the signal, I would take one step back, increasing the length of her jump.

I wanted to ask, "You're not really going to jump, are you? You can't jump. You don't have enough strength in your body to pull it off," but I didn't say a word. I kept my thoughts to myself.

I moved in close, about six inches from the counter. "If you want to jump, Daddy will catch you," I said.

Jackie raised her little right hand and motioned for me to move back further, away from the counter.

I was awestruck and dumbfounded.

I started to well up with tears, but I didn't want her to see me cry. I stepped back six inches. Normally, I would have stepped back a foot, but I wanted to be close enough in case she just fell straight down from the edge of the counter. She motioned again for me to move back further. I worried that if I took another step back, she would land on the floor and suffer an injury.

However, she believed it was possible. In fact, she looked so confident and that look convinced me to do it her way. I stepped back six more inches. She motioned a third time to move back further. Now, we were moving from the unimaginable to the absurd. I couldn't hide the tears at this point. I again took one small step back.

Without any warning, she jumped off the counter. In reality, she just fell straightforward. I was close enough to lean forward and catch her in my arms. I hugged her for all it was worth. I kissed her little head and held her up in the air. "Jackie, Daddy's so proud of you. That was amazing," I said with joy. She had the biggest smile on her face as we laughed together.

Standing up and jumping off that kitchen counter was the most courageous act I have ever witnessed. It was inconceivable that she was able to pull it off. I'll never forget that moment. It became a watershed moment, a turning point in my life. I realized that we are all capable of so much more than we think. Jackie's strength amid hardship gave me a motivation to "go for it" in life. She is my hero, inspiration, and the wind beneath my wings.

TO TURN YOUR PAIN INTO PURPOSE

As I reflect on that moment, the phrase, "Jackie Power," echoes in my mind. Despite everything, she had an unstoppable power in her soul. She willed herself to stand and jump. She believed it was possible and she made it happen.

For me, *Jackie Power* represents the power I have within myself that comes from God. She was a life force and awakened me to God's power. It's another way of saying, "I can do all things through Christ who strengthens me" (Philippians 4:13 NKJV).

God gave Jackie the strength to jump off that counter one last time. Whenever I think I don't have enough strength, I call upon my Jackie Power. Her example of courage inspires me to overcome any fear, challenge, or obstacle I face. We all have Jackie Power if we tap into it and believe in the possibilities. Are you aware of the God-given life force you have within you?

My Jackie Power started with weightlifting. I was lifting some heavy weights on the bench press with a goal of doing six repetitions. On the sixth rep, my arms started to shake and I didn't think I could get the bar up. I pictured Jackie in my mind struggling to stand on the counter and finally stranding erect. The thought gave me a shot of adrenaline as I pushed the bar all the way up.

I felt led to go back to school and get an MBA degree. I was now in my forties. The idea of studying and writing two papers a week for a couple of years was daunting. I enrolled in the

MBA program at the Ken Blanchard School of Business at Grand Canyon University. It was a grueling program that stretched me to the limit. Three months in, I felt overwhelmed and wanted to quit. As I was about to throw in the towel, I thought of Jackie, her tenacity and courage, and I powered through.

I enrolled in a doctorate program at Biola University in my early fifties. The final project was to write a 250-page dissertation. I didn't think I could do it, but I remembered Jackie's act of courage. I completed the dissertation and graduated recently with my doctorate.

I was recently diagnosed with leukemia. I was shocked and scared. I have CLL, chronic lymphocytic leukemia, a terminal blood cancer. I once again thought of Jackie and my perspective changed. I began to tell myself, "I am living with leukemia, not dying with leukemia."

I've always wanted to write a book and now you are reading it. I'm doing so much more than I had ever imagined was possible.

What a gift Jackie gave me the day she jumped off the kitchen counter. I am now willing to venture outside my comfort zone, attempt big projects, and achieve things I never dreamed possible. All of this because of a little girl with a brain tumor who wouldn't give up. She fought for every moment of fun. Her accomplishments may seem tiny to you, but they're on a grand scale to me.

In the next chapter in *The School of Grief*, you will learn about the final need grievers have: the hope of heaven after we die and being united with our loved ones.

CHAPTER 15:
TO HOLD ONTO THE HOPE OF HEAVEN

> *"We may speak about a place where there are no tears, no death, no fear, no night; but those are just the benefits of heaven. The beauty of heaven is seeing God."*
> *Max Lucado*

The seventh and final need for those who grieve is our need for an afterlife and being reunited with our loved ones. Heaven is the ultimate hope for every believer, to "dwell in the house of the Lord forever" (Psalm 23:6). We need to hold onto the hope for heaven.

A recent study found nearly three-quarters of U.S. adults say they believe in heaven. Two-thirds of U.S. adults believe that deceased people are reunited with loved ones in heaven.[1] And yet there are many people who do not believe in an afterlife. Some believe in oblivion after death, while others believe an individual is reborn into this world and begins the life cycle over again, likely with no memory of what they have done in the past.

A Glimpse of Heaven

Jackie loved animals and always wanted a hamster as a pet. My wife and I are not fans of the rodent, especially living in our home. But Jackie was going to die soon, so I said, "What the heck?" Sometimes, that's just what you need to say.

Carrie assigned me the task of going to the pet store with Jackie to let her pick out a hamster. It turned out to be the greatest job I ever had. I don't think I've ever seen Jackie more excited. We drove to a large pet store in Roseville, and she carefully examined all the hamsters, picking up most of them. She finally chose one baby brown and white dwarf hamster. It was a girl. She named her Emily.

Jackie held Emily on our drive home from the pet store. It was a sunny day. The sunroof on my Volvo was open and the sun was shining down on us.

Out of the blue, Jackie turned and looked at me quizzically. "Daddy, when I get to heaven, will I see Jesus right away?" she asked.

"Yes, you will, sweetie," I replied. I assured her that she would indeed see Jesus immediately.

She smiled. A few seconds later, she asked, "When I get to heaven, will I get to see Grandpa?"

Her grandpa, my dad, had passed away a year earlier. She really loved him, and it was the first time Jackie ever lost someone she loved. I assured her that she would get to see Grandpa in heaven and be reunited with him.

Then, she paused for a moment, turned and looked at me while holding Emily in her right hand, and asked, "Daddy, can I take Emily with me to heaven?"

The first two questions were easy. This one was a bit more difficult to answer. I thought for a moment. I knew the correct theological answer, but I responded, "Yes, Jackie, you can take Emily with you to heaven; we can arrange that." She grinned from ear to ear.

I thought to myself, *What's going on here?* So, I looked over at her and asked, "Sweetie, you don't really think you're going to die, do you?"

She looked at me, smiled, and said, "Silly daddy, we are all going to die someday."

Wow. Her answer took my breath away. God was giving Jackie a glimpse of heaven. She had a spiritual sixth sense that she was going to be arriving in heaven soon. She would be leaving our home, which she dearly loved, to go to her ultimate eternal home in heaven, and she was okay with that.

I will never forget that conversation as long as I live. Over the years, I have reflected on this brief conversation more than any conversation I have ever had with anyone. Her response still fascinates me and brings me great comfort.

Looking back, I believe God was preparing my baby girl for what she was about to face by giving her some glimpses of what heaven would be like. As her transition day approached when she would pass from this life to the next, instead of being afraid, Jackie was ready to go to heaven, meet Jesus, and be reunited with her grandpa.

For only being five years old, Jackie had a deep curiosity about heaven. She asked Carrie if angels were going to accompany her to heaven. "Absolutely," Carrie said. Again, God was preparing Jackie for her journey to eternity.

God Put Eternity into Every Human Heart

Have you ever felt like there is something else after death? C.S. Lewis said, "If we find ourselves with a desire that nothing in this world can satisfy, the most probable explanation is that we were made for another world."

The band, Switchfoot, echoed this thought in a song called *Meant to Live*:

"We want more than this world's got to offer We want more than the wars of our fathers And everything inside screams for second life We were meant to live for so much more."[2]

The wise King Solomon wrote that God has "set eternity in the human heart" (Ecclesiastes 3:11). And with this awareness of eternity comes a hope that we can one day find a fulfillment that is not afforded by the vanities in this world.

"In the human heart" is talking about our mind, soul, and spirit. I believe we are spiritual beings, first and foremost, that live in physical bodies. Our spirit is eternal while our bodies on this earth are temporal. Yet we will receive new bodies in heaven (2 Corinthians 5:1-5). Solomon says God places eternity into our heart and soul. The word "eternity" is the Hebrew word *olam*, referring to an eternal longing within the human heart. I believe this longing is twofold. It's a longing to know God and it's a longing to spend eternity with God in heaven.

A Longing to Know God

This longing to know God is expressed by St. Augustine in his *Confessions*, "Thou hast formed us for Thyself, and our hearts are restless till they find rest in Thee." Animals don't have a longing to know God or for heaven. Humans possess an innate knowledge that there is something more to life than what we can see and experience in the here and now.

Psalm 42:1-2 says, "As the deer pants for streams of water, so my soul pants for you, O God. My soul thirsts for God, for the living God" (Psalm 42:1-2). Jesus said, "Come to me, all who labor and are heavy laden, and I will give you rest" (Matthew 11:28).

Jesus knows how burdened we can get in this life and offers an open invitation to anyone who is laboring under a heavy toll and seeks rest for their soul. Who better to carry our load of grief than Jesus? He can carry what you are not able to carry.

Over the Rainbow

Our longing for heaven is exemplified in a song, voted the song of the century, none other than *Over the Rainbow*, which was sung by Judy Garland in the movie *The Wizard of Oz*. The lyrics were written by Yip Harbug, the son of Russian-Jewish immigrants. His real name is Isidore Hochberg. What you may not know is that the first verse of the original tune was omitted from the movie. The popular version starts with the chorus. Songs don't normally start with the chorus but this one does. Here are the lyrics to the original song that you've probably never heard before:

"When all the world is a hopeless jumble, and the raindrops tumble, all around,
Heaven opens a magic lane.
When all the clouds darken up the sky way, there's a rainbow highway to be found.
Leading from your windowpane to a place behind the sun,
Just a step beyond the rain.
Then the song goes into the chorus:
"Somewhere over the rainbow, Way up high
There's a land that I heard of Once in a lullaby.
Somewhere over the rainbow
Skies are blue
And the dreams that you dare to dream really do come true."

The song is about hope. It's called *Over the Rainbow*. God created rainbows as a sign of hope. This song speaks of a yearning for another place, a better place; but there is a sadness in the realization that this place isn't situated on earth. Somewhere over the rainbow is a great description of heaven, a place where our dreams really do come true.

Heaven is Our Home

I always wanted to get a dog—a big dog! But there were always problems. Either our home was too small or the kids were too young. The main problem, however, was the lack of enthusiasm on

the part of my wife because from her perspective, she had one slobbering shedding beast, and she didn't need another one.

Now, I realize what I'm about to say is going to offend some of you but here goes: Small dogs are not real dogs. Small dogs don't bark; they yelp. They don't eat; they nibble.

TO HOLD ONTO THE HOPE OF HEAVEN

They don't lick you; they just sniff you. I wanted a real dog, a man's best friend kind of dog.

And then came Ari. Ari is a pure breed Siberian Husky, black and white with blue eyes. Ari was a gorgeous dog we got from a family in Santa Clarita. My daughter, Jessica, picked her out of the litter. So, we gave her a name and cleared out a place in our house where she would live. Before Ari was born, she had been claimed and named and a place had been prepared for her.

Sound familiar? Before you were born, you were named by God; you had been claimed by God, and a place had been prepared for you. And while you're here, another place is being prepared for you. That's what the breeder did with Ari. We had to wait six weeks before we could take possession of Ari because the breeder wanted to wean her and train her a little bit.

God is weaning us from earthly affections and is training us for our new home. He has prepared a place for us. At some point, we'll do what Ari did. Ari traveled from her home in Santa Clarita ultimately to our home. We, too, will go to from this earth to our home in heaven. We don't know our departure date and we don't know our flight number, but you can bet your puppy chow that it won't be long until you see your master's face!

This is the promise Paul gave us in Philippians 3:20-21: "But our citizenship is in heaven. And we eagerly await a Savior from there, the Lord Jesus Christ, who, by the power that enables him to bring everything under his control, will transform our lowly bodies so that they will be like his glorious body."

Paul says our true citizenship is in heaven. One translation says, "Our homeland is in heaven." There truly is no place like home when heaven is your home. Every believer has a divinely implanted awareness that our souls live forever. This world is not our home; we are only passing through this life on earth. Songwriter Bob Sobo wrote these lyrics in his song *Heaven is My Home*: "My trust is not in earthly things to satisfy my soul; my hope is set in Christ my king and heaven is my home."

Jesus Overcomes Death Through His Resurrection

Jesus promised, "I am the resurrection and the life. He who believes in me, though he may die, he shall live. And whoever lives and believes in me shall never die" (John 11:25-26). The Bible links sin with death. It says, "The sting of death is sin" (1 Corinthians 15:56) and "through one man sin entered the world, and death through sin, and thus death spread to all men, because all sinned" (Romans 5:12).

Death stalks the rich and the poor, the educated and the uneducated. Death is no respecter of persons. Its shadow haunts us day and night. We never know when the moment of death will come for us.

In the resurrection of Jesus Christ, we have the answer to the great question of the ages originally posed by Job: "If a man dies, shall he live again?" (Job 14:14). The Bible teaches that because Christ lives, we also shall live. The greatest truth we will ever hear is that Jesus Christ died and rose again, and that you, too, will die but can rise again into newness of life.

The only hope we have for dealing with death is the resurrection of Jesus and it's the only hope we need. The Bible teaches the bodily resurrection of Jesus Christ. It is not a spiritual resurrection, as some would have us believe. Jesus' physical body was raised by God from the dead, and someday, we will see him.

Since Jesus died and rose again, death cannot separate us from the love of God. Paul said, "For I am convinced that neither death nor life ... will be able to separate us from the love of God that is in Christ Jesus our Lord" (Romans 8:38-39).

When Jesus died, death was destroyed. Satan, the one who holds the power of death, will someday also be destroyed. Death and sin no longer have mastery. This is why Paul says, "Where, O death, is your victory? Where, O death, is your sting?" The death of Christ means victory for those who believe in Him. Eternal life and immortality come to all those who believe in him.

The Reality of Heaven

To be absent from the body is to be present with the Lord (2 Corinthians 5:8). The moment we take our last breath on earth, we take our first in heaven. Heaven is a wonderful place but there are several misconceptions about what heaven is like. You won't become an angel, and neither will your lost loved one. You won't have wings. You're not going to be a little chubby cherub, wearing a white robe and floating on clouds.

Below are four realities about heaven:[3]

Heaven is where God lives. The Bible calls heaven "the dwelling place of God." Billy Graham said, "The most thrilling thing about heaven is that Jesus Christ will be there. I will see Him face to face. Jesus Christ will meet us at the end of life's journey."

Heaven is where God rules. Jesus calls heaven "the Kingdom of God," so heaven isn't just where God lives; it's also where he rules. The Psalmist wrote, "Lord, I look up to you, up to heaven, where you rule" (Psalm 123:1 GNT).

Heaven is a literal place. Heaven isn't a state of mind or a state of being. The Scripture says there will be streets, trees, water, and homes in heaven. Some Scripture passages allude to the fact that animals are there. You'll have your physical body, renewed through your resurrection. And there will be a real place for your real body to live. Jesus said, "There are many rooms in my Father's house. I wouldn't tell you this unless it was true. I am going there to prepare a place for each of you" (John 14:2 CEV).

Heaven is designed for his followers. God didn't design heaven for Himself. Jesus said, "Come, you who are blessed by my Father; take your inheritance, the kingdom prepared for you" (Matthew 25:34).

Heaven is a place God designed for His family, and heaven is an expression of His love. People aren't meant to live on earth forever. You and I were made for heaven! Hebrews 13:14 says, "For this world is not our home; we are looking forward to our everlasting home in heaven" (Hebrews 13:14 TLB). The Apostle Paul wrote, "No eye has seen, no ear has heard, and no mind has imagined what God has prepared for those who love him" (1 Corinthians 2:9 NLT).

Absence Makes the Heart Grow Fonder

The absence of our loved one has allowed us to tap into a new depth of love, one we didn't know even existed until their loss. I believe *yearning*, an intense longing for what we lost, is the most dominant feeling after a loss, more than the typical emotions associated with grief. This absence is a depth of love we couldn't access while they were still alive. It's a love built on the void they left in the world when they passed. In the gap between what I couldn't ever imagine and my present reality lies a type of love I met for the first time in my grief. It's a void I couldn't have imagined before she passed.

When Jackie died, her *absence* became its own presence. It represented all that is gone, all that I loved, and all that I missed. I hate the reality it represents but I also love the reality it represents: that my love for her is so great that she is still here, even though she is no longer physically here. I grab hold of her absence and cling to it as tightly as possible. I visit our memories, knowing they hold both the deepest joy and deepest pain.

With Jackie's absence, I learned something I couldn't know while she was still living. I learned just how deeply I was capable of missing her. I learned how much pain her void in my life could cause. And I learned how willing I am to lean into that pain to keep her close. I still feel connected with her, still talk to her, and in my prayers, I ask God to give her a hug for me.

I marvel at the depth of my love because of her loss. But deep down in my soul, I want to see her again and have the pain cease.

Reunited with Our Loved Ones

The hope of heaven and being reunited with my daughter is a thrilling certainty that will completely satisfy the yearning I have in my heart to see her again. The hope of being reunited with our loved ones brings tremendous comfort to those of us on earth who have lost a loved one.

King David lost his newborn son to illness but said with confidence: "He will not return to me but (one day) I will go to him" (2 Samuel 12:23). Jackie will not come back here to earth, but I am confident I will one day go and be reunited with her in heaven. We will recognize our loved ones in heaven, even though my daughter was only five years old when she passed.

Someday soon, I will be reunited with all those in my family who are already there, including my daughter. And when that happens, we will fellowship around our Father's throne, finally meeting

him face-to-face. And the family of God, our brothers, and sisters in Christ, will be there. What an emotional reunion it will be! Our yearnings will be satisfied.

Conclusion

My oldest daughter, Jessica, wrote a poem about heaven and Jackie when she was 12 years old, five years after Jackie passed. The poem is simply called *Heaven*.

Heaven
By Jessica Page

Mommy, what's wrong with me?
My head hurts so bad.
You take me to the doctor's and tell me that I'm sick.
Why do you and Daddy look so sad?

I don't want any more radiation, Mommy.
Please get me out of this place.
I want to talk to you, but my mouth won't move.
All I can do is watch your crying face.

Mommy, I can laugh and smile again!
Guess who I can see?
Jesus is calling me towards Heaven.
You always said it is such a great place to be.

Mommy, I'm getting closer now.
I'm walking through big golden gates.
Stop crying for me Mommy cause I will see you again.
And I will be happy up here as I wait.

Jackie loved announcing to the neighborhood that Daddy was home and then jumping into my arms. She enjoyed climbing onto the kitchen counter and asking me to back up so she could take a flying leap into my arms.

At the end of her battle with cancer, she was able to stand one last time and jump into my arms. In the same way she jumped into my arms as her earthly father, I picture her jumping into her Heavenly Father's waiting arms.

My baby is now in heaven, safe in the arms of God.

The Apostle John said, "I heard a loud voice from the throne saying, 'Look! God's dwelling place is now among the people, and he will dwell with them'" (Revelation 21:3). God is always with us. God became human in Jesus and is called our *Immanuel*, which means, "God with us." Jesus came to earth to heal the brokenhearted.

Our comfort comes in knowing we are not alone. God is fully present with us in our pain and loss. He wraps His arms around us and whispers in our ears, "I love you."

Irish poet Thomas Moore said, "Earth has no sorrow that heaven cannot heal."

The first followers of Jesus spoke about a day in the future when God would restore everything—you, me, everything in heaven and on earth. (Acts 3:21). The resurrection of Jesus conquered our greatest enemy, death itself, and points to a day when all those in Christ will be raised again to live forever with him in heaven and be united with the people we love.

On that day, the Apostle said, "He (God) will wipe every tear from their eyes, and there will be no more death or sorrow or crying or pain. All these things are gone forever. Look, I am making everything new!" (Revelation 21:4). God is making everything new, including you.

May you hold onto the hope of heaven and realize God is sitting Shiva with you, fully present, grieving your loss. But also restoring everything. And in that, we find hope.

ENDNOTES

Chapter 3: Will My Life Ever Be Good Again?

1. Jerry Sittser, *A Grace Disguised: How the Soul Grows Through Loss. Expanded Edition (Grand Rapids, MI:* Zondervan, 1995, 2004), 202.

2. David Kessler, *Finding Meaning: The Sixth Stage of Grief* (New York, NY: Simon & Schuster, 2019), 33.

3. Elisabeth Kübler-Ross & David Kessler *on Grief and Grieving: Finding the Meaning of Grief Through the Five Stages of Loss* (New York, NY: Scribner, 2005), 230.

Chapter 4: What is Grief?

1. Sheryl Sandberg & Adam Grant, *Option B: Facing Adversity, Building Resilience, and Finding Joy* (New York, NY: Penguin Random House, 2017), 13.

2. Etymology of the word *grief* from Vocabulary.com. https://www.vocabulary.com/dictionary/grief

3. David Kessler, David Kessler Training Video, "Understanding Grief," *Grief.com*

4. Mary Frances O'Connor, *The Grieving Brain: The Surprising Science of How We Learn from Love and Loss* (San Francisco, CA: HarperOne, 2022). O'Conner discusses the difference between grief and grieving.

5. Larry Hendren, "Peeling the Onion: A Simple Primer on Grief," *Simmons Chaplain Services* (February 9, 2017).

6. Doug Manning, The Journey of Grief DVD, "The Dimensions of Grief," *InSight Books*, (2007).

7. Ibid.

8. Reddit Online Forum. "My friend just died. I don't know what to do." Reddit Post reply by GSnow that 2,700 people read and liked. https://www.reddit.com/r/Assistance/comments/hax0t/

Chapter 5: Models of Grief

1. Elisabeth Kübler-Ross, *On Death and Dying* (New York, NY: Scribner, 1969), 12.

2. Rick Warren, "How to Get Through What You're Going Through." An 8-Week Sermon Series on the 6 Stages of Grief. *Pastors.com* (July 2013).

3. J. William Worden, *Grief Counseling and Grief Therapy: A Handbook for the Mental Health Practitioner. Fourth Edition* (New York: NY: Springer Publishing, 2009), 39-52.

Chapter 6: The Best and Worst Things to Say

1. Kay Warren, "Don't Tell Me to Move On." *Facebook.com/KayWarrensPage* (April 5, 2014).

2. Doug Manning, *The Funeral: A Chance to Touch. A Chance to Serve. A Chance to Heal* (Oklahoma City, OK: InSight Books, 2001), 100.

Chapter 7: Faith and Grief

1. A.W. Tozer, *The Knowledge of the Holy: The Attributes of God: Their Meaning in the Christian Life* (San Francisco, CA: Harper & Row, 1961), 1.

2. Bill Hybels, *Romans 8: Inseparable: New Community Bible Study Series* (Grand Rapids, MI: Zondervan, 2009), 45.

Chapter 8: The 7 Needs of the Grieving

1. John W. James & Russell Friedman, *The Grief Recovery Handbook: 20th Anniversary* (New York, NY: HarperCollins, 2009), 26-37.

Chapter 9: To Have Your Grief Witnessed

1. David Kessler, *Finding Meaning: The Sixth Stage of Grief* (New York, NY: Simon & Schuster, 2019), 29.

2. Ibid, 30.

3. Doug Manning, *The Gift of Significance* (Oklahoma City, OK: InSight Books, 1992), 49-52.

4. David Kessler, *Finding Meaning: The Sixth Stage of Grief* (New York, NY: Simon & Schuster, 2019), 34.

ENDNOTES

Chapter 10: To Feel the Feelings

1. Laird Hamilton was quoted saying, "Do the laps" when training for big wave surfing from the documentary *Take Every Wave: The Life of Laird Hamilton*, (2017). Available on Apple TV.

2. Paul Brand & Philip Yancey, *The Gift of Pain: Why We Hurt and What We Can Do About It* (Grand Rapids, MI: Zondervan, 1997), 6.

3. Ann B. Weems, *Psalms of Lament* (Louisville, KY: Westminster John Knox Press, 1995). An excerpt called, "Jesus Wept."

4. Judith Orloff, "The Health Benefit of Tears," *Psychology Today* (July 27, 2010). Dr. Orloff discussed how tears can benefit our health by giving research from biochemist and *tear expert* Dr. William Frey. https://www.psychologytoday.com/us/blog/emotional-freedom/201007/the-health-benefits-tears

Chapter 11: To Release the Burden of Guilt

1. Eric Moore, "The Tragedy of Eric Clapton: How the Loss of His Son Changed His Life Forever," *FuelRocks.com Blog* (February 3, 2023), https://www.fuelrocks.com/the-tragedy-of-eric-clapton-how-the-loss-of-his-son-changed-his-life-forever/

2. Matthew Boland, "Is Guilt a Natural Aspect of Grief?" *PsychCentral.com* (September 21, 2022). https://psychcentral.com/health/grief-and-guilt

Chapter 12: To Face Your Fears

1. Rory Vanden, "Buffalo Charge the Storm," *RoyVanden.com Blog* (August 17, 2022). https://roryvaden.com/blog/leadership/buffalo-charge-the-storm-story-by-rory-vaden/

2. Jerry Sittser, *A Grace Disguised: How the Soul Grows Through Loss* (Grand Rapids, MI: Zondervan, 1995), 33.

Chapter 13: To Not Get Over It – But Grow Into It

1. Jerry Sittser, *A Grace Disguised: How the Soul Grows Through Loss* (Grand Rapids, MI: Zondervan, 1995), 46.

2. Viktor E. Frankl, *Man's Search for Meaning* (Boston, MA: Beacon Press, 1959), 66.

3. David Jeremiah, "Finding Your Purpose Through Pain: The Story of Joni Earekson Tada" *DavidJeremiah.Blog*

https://davidjeremiah.blog/finding-your-purpose-through-pain-the-story-of-joni-eareckson-tada/

4. John W. James & Russell Friedman, *The Grief Recovery Handbook: 20th Anniversary* (New York, NY: HarperCollins, 2009), 26-37.

Chapter 14: To Turn Your Pain Into Purpose

1. John C. Maxwell, *Intentional Living: Choosing a Life That Matters* (New York, NY: Center Street, 2015), 92-99.

2. Louis Evely. *Suffering.* (New York, NY: Herder and Herder, 1967), 69.

Chapter 15: To Hold Onto the Hope of Heaven

1. Pew Research Center, "Views of the Afterlife," *PewResearch.org* (November 23, 2021).
https://www.pewresearch.org/religion/2021/11/23/views-on-the-afterlife/

2. Jon Foreman, Singer & Songwriter of the song *Meant to Live* on the album The Beautiful Letdown. Recorded in 2003 by the band Switchfoot on the Columbia label.

3. Rick Warren, "Three Realities of Heaven." Daily Hope Devotionals, *PastorRick.com* (September 25, 2022).
https://pastorrick.com/three-realities-of-heaven/

TRANSLATIONS

All Scripture quotations, unless otherwise indicated, are taken from the *Holy Bible, New International Version (NIV)*. Copyright © 1973,1978, 1984 by International Bible Society. Used by permission of Zondervan. All rights reserved. Other Bible translations used include:

AMP *The Amplified Bible*
  Grand Rapids: Zondervan (1965)

CEV *Contemporary English Version*
  New York: American Bible Society (1995)

GWT *God's Word Translation*
  Grand Rapids: World Publishing, Inc. (1995)

KJV *King James Version*

LB *Living Bible*
  Wheaton, IL: Tyndale House Publishers (1979)

MSG *The Message*
  Colorado Springs: Navpress (1993)

NASB *New American Standard Bible*
  Anaheim, CA: Foundation Press (1973)

NKJV *New King James Version*

NLT *New Living Translation*
  Wheaton, IL: Tyndale House Publishers (1996)

ABOUT THE AUTHOR

Dr. David Page is the Director of Pastoral Care at Shepherd Church, an influential and racially diverse church in Los Angeles. He previously served as a care pastor at Saddleback Church, one of America's largest churches. He is a grief educator and coach, trained by David Kessler, arguably the foremost expert in the world on grief and loss. Dave is also an author, public speaker, and a funeral celebrant that worked with Forest Lawn Memorial-Parks walking alongside hundreds of families by performing memorial services for their loved ones.

Dave is known as the grief pastor at Shepherd Church. He started a grief ministry called *Hope for Grief* and trains pastors on how to do memorials and minister to people in pain. Dave also started an online grief support community called *Compassionate Hearts*. He worked beside Saddleback's founding pastor, Rick Warren, and his wife, Kay, as both mentors and friends, witnessing firsthand how they responded with grief and grace after losing their son to suicide.

Dave is a lifelong learner and earned a doctorate degree in ministry from Biola University, two master's degrees, and a bachelor's degree. One of his hobbies includes basketball. He played in high school and college and wanted to play guard for the Lakers. He didn't grow up wanting to be a pastor or grief educator. He didn't choose his career; it chose him, and he loves it. He's married to his beautiful wife, Carrie, has three kids, and lives in Southern California.

www.pastordave.com
www.schoolofgrief.com

School of Grief Publishing
Dr. David E. Page
19700 Rinaldi Street, Porter Ranch, CA 91326
(818) 831-9333

Cover design: Yasir Nadeem
Interior formatting: Aeysha
Photo of author: Christian Del Rosario
Photo of Jackie: Jennifer Smith

Printed in the United States of America

Made in the USA
Las Vegas, NV
16 September 2023